brilliant
NLP

D1387011

brilliant NLP

What the most successful people
know, say and do

David Molden and
Pat Hutchinson

Harlow, England • London • New York • Boston • San Francisco • Toronto
Sydney • Tokyo • Singapore • Hong Kong • Seoul • Taipei • New Delhi
Cape Town • Madrid • Mexico City • Amsterdam • Munich • Paris • Milan

PEARSON EDUCATION LIMITED

Edinburgh Gate
Harlow CM20 2JE
Tel: +44 (0)1279 623623
Fax: +44 (0)1279 431059
Website: www.pearsoned.co.uk

First published in Great Britain in 2006

ISBN-13: 978-0-273-70789-9

British Library Cataloguing-in-Publication Data
A catalogue record for this book is available from the British Library.

Library of Congress Cataloging-in-Publication Data
Molden David
    Brilliant NLP : what the most successful people know, say, and do / David Molden
and Pat Hutchinson.
        p. cm.
    ISBN-13: 978-0-273-70789-9 (alk. paper)

    1. Neurolinguistic programming. I. Title: Brilliant neurolinguistic programming.
II. Hutchinson, Pat. III. Title.

    BF637.N46M65 2006
    158.1—dc22

                                                                            2006041687

10 9 8 7 6 5
10 09 08 07

Cartoons by Bill Piggins
Typeset in 10/14pt Latin 725 by 70
Printed and bound in Great Britain

The publisher's policy is to use paper manufactured from sustainable forests.

Contents

Acknowledgements

We would like to thank all the people who have helped and supported us in the writing of this book – friends, family and the publishing team at Pearson Education. There are many more without whom this book would not have been possible – all the people mentioned in this book whose names we have changed and who have achieved such great things with NLP. Our intention is that you will join them by having wonderful experiences in your life through the power of NLP. Enjoy.

Introduction

NLP can change your life. It is a remarkable force for change. We know this because we've seen it happen with many, many people over many years.

As a result of using NLP, we've seen people bring their dreams to life and make huge things happen – career and life crises solved; managers bringing about radical change in their companies; couples finding happiness after realizing what is really important to them; teachers finding new ways to motivate children to learn; entrepreneurs operating at world-class levels; people changing the way they are perceived by others. In short, we've watched people use what they've learned to become more successful in everything they do. These people are the reason we know that NLP is *Brilliant* – it has given so many the tools and techniques to take huge strides forward in their personal and professional lives, and you can join them.

What is NLP and what can it do for me?

NLP is a set of tools and techniques to help you deal with unhelpful patterns of thought and behaviour (some you won't even know you have) and to introduce new, positive and constructive ways to improve your life. Although there are many tools and techniques in NLP, you don't need to learn them all to get started and *gain immediate benefit*. You can make amazing changes by using just one technique – simply use the exercises to experience what NLP has to offer and prepare to be astounded by the results.

A bit of history

NLP was created by Dr Richard Bandler and Dr John Grinder in the early 70s in California. Bandler and Grinder have long since gone their separate ways, but have continued to develop NLP models and techniques. In the last 30 years or so, many others have contributed to this evolving field of personal change – too many to mention here. Our recent contribution can be found in the development of 'This not That' in the section on reframing at the end of Chapter 3. Bandler and Grinder wanted to discover how successful people achieve their results and then to learn how to replicate their models. They began by modelling highly effective therapists but moved on to sales executives, negotiators, public speakers, trainers and leaders. Very soon they had drawn together the very best personal change tools from a variety of disciplines, plus models of excellence from their early subjects, and they designed the very first public training in NLP. Today NLP offers a vast array of effective tools and techniques for positive influence and change.

It does what it says on the can

The letters 'NLP' stand for neurolinguistic programming. If you break down the name, it helps explain what it's all about:

- 'neuro' refers to the brain and nervous system;
- 'linguistic' is the verbal and non-verbal language used to communicate;
- 'programming' is the unique way you put all this together to create your behaviour.

You have one brain but two minds – one conscious and the other unconscious. When you get out of bed in the morning you begin running programmes stored in the depths of your unconscious mind – the one that remembers how to do all the things you do automatically: how to ride a bicycle, how to drive a car, how to make yourself feel good and how to make yourself feel bad. This storage area is much larger than the conscious mind you are using to read this book right now. The two minds work in cooperation, a typical example being when you are reading and your conscious mind suddenly switches to something else.

Your unconscious mind takes over the reading and you arrive at the foot of the page not remembering anything about what you have just read. Once formed, a programme has the capacity for amazing consistency producing the same results over and over again. Some programmes will work well for you, while others may have undesirable results and be holding you back. NLP is used to change the programmes that are not working and create new ones that do.

For most people things happen and they react. NLP offers a better way. It gives you the tools to react differently by choice, and to be more aware of your thoughts, feelings and behaviour. You will discover what really makes you tick, and begin to make crystal clear decisions about what you want from work and life. Only you can take responsibility for your results and make changes to improve the quality of your life. It's like taking firm hold of the steering wheel used to direct your career and personal life where you decide to go using a real sense of vision and determination. Once you have it you can use it to generate brilliant results in all areas of your life.

How well do you know yourself?

Have you ever wondered how it is that two people facing the same set of circumstances can produce diametrically opposite results? How some people seem to be able to achieve infinitely more than others? You may also have noticed how some people have a tendency to attract lively vibrant people while others are very good at attracting moaners and groaners. There are people who seem to have life sorted out just the way they want it, and others who are either surviving or struggling with frequent problems and difficulties. So what makes the difference?

Successful people are often thought of as lucky – but is it really luck? Luck infers that there is some form of gambling involved, but on close inspection these people show few signs of taking chances with their lives. Anyway, the sheer consistency with which they achieve good results would defy the laws of gambling. No, it has more to do with **the way they think**. Taking control of your thinking is key in the pursuit of success. To do this you first need to realize the impact your thinking is having on your life. You may think that circumstances beyond your control are keeping you where you are, like a frog in a well who thinks the small circle of blue sky above is all there is outside the well. Not until he clings to the bucket for the journey skyward does he realize how much more there is out there. The techniques used in NLP are designed to increase your awareness and, as a consequence, your choices in life.

1 Think your way to success

Imagine your mind is like a kaleidoscope, which has been left to form its own patterns over the years. Sometimes it falls one way and a pattern forms. Some time later the kaleidoscope is knocked and it rolls into a different position, so the pattern changes and settles there for a while. Maybe this continues for a number of years until one day you decide to pick up the kaleidoscope and take control of pattern making. With one small twist the whole colour scheme changes and forms a completely new and more exciting pattern. Twist again and another one appears and so on. The real challenge now is to decide which of the patterns is the most beautiful – or, in terms of thought patterns, the most useful, empowering and enabling. So what is inside the kaleidoscope that makes up so many different patterns?

What are you storing in your unconscious mind and how useful is it?

Your patterns, in the kaleidoscope, represent how you think about yourself and your experiences including:

■ values
  - what's important to you personally
  - the value you place on people, things, places, activities and information
  - your intrinsic values (also called metaprogrammes)

- beliefs
  - what you believe about yourself and others
  - your opinions, judgements and capacity for conjecture.

What is important to you?

What is really important in your life? How about your work? What is it about your work that makes all the effort you put in worthwhile? What's important about your relationship with your partner, your immediate and extended family, friends and colleagues? When you ask these questions of yourself where do your answers come from? Do they come from your head or your heart? These are your values – the things in life that are really important to you and which you will go out of your way to protect, uphold and defend.

So do you know, with conviction, what is important to you? Does the tone of voice in which you answer these questions match the words you use to describe what is important? Or does it suggest that what you consider to be important to you is really an obligation? There is a big difference between a value born out of obligation and one born out of choice. This is a question you probably ask yourself rarely, yet the answer provides an insight as to why you may be dissatisfied with certain areas of your life. You may think that the way to a fulfilled career and life is through setting goals, making a plan and getting on with it. If it were really that easy wouldn't everyone be doing it?

Many of the things that are important to you are not even in your conscious awareness. They are not so easily rationalized, and while you are busy chasing a career, money, partner, happiness or some kind of recognition the important things and people can get lost. What's important to you has a big impact on the way you behave. So if you feel that circumstances are forcing you to do things which go against your values then you will feel an uncomfortable tug somewhere in your body. You may not know where it comes from, what is causing it or even what it is about. Such tugs appear in many different forms – it could be a feeling of discomfort, a fleeting thought or unpleasant memory or a shiver. The chances are that you will ignore them and move on, but this is your unconscious mind giving you a signal that something demands your attention. You can ignore it for so long but if you continue then you are suppressing the real you and your inherent energy. When energy becomes blocked it can ultimately cause illness and disease. It makes sense to pay attention to tugs.

Where do your values come from?

You will have gathered values all your life, starting from the day you were born, and will have carried some of them with you into adulthood. What are they? How did you get them? What influence are they having on you?

- **Inherited values** are possibly the most common. As a child you will have been influenced by what was important to your parents, siblings, extended family, teachers and group leaders. Later on you will have become a little more selective, adapting the values of your chosen heroes from the worlds of sport, fashion, film, music, politics and so on. By the time you reached adulthood your values were already forming a major part of your adult programmes. For example, if you were always told to finish your food at meal-times you may now be eating much more than you need. If your parents were very academic you may put a high value on acquiring formal qualifications.

- **Compensatory values** are formed when you go to the other extreme to compensate for something which didn't happen for you. For example, if you had a deprived childhood you may compensate for this by overindulging your own children.

- **Your own judgements**, or the way you perceive your own experiences will have an impact on the value you place on them. If you have ever been burgled or robbed you are likely to place a high value on security, which may not be appropriate in some circumstances.

On the surface these values may seem innocent enough. However, under closer inspection it is surprising what a major role they play in determining the way your life pans out. When you recognize an uncomfortable tug, a feeling that all is not well, examine your values to determine whether what you are doing is violating a deeply held value. Use the following technique to discover your true values and to make choices that will serve you well.

Discover your true values

Step 1

Think back to a time when you last felt a tug – was it to do with a relationship, your work, your family, your finances or your self-esteem and confidence? Then answer the questions

- 'What is important to me about ....?
  (complete with the subject of your tug)

- 'What else is important to me about ....?

For example you might start with 'What is important to me about my job?' and follow up with 'What else is important to me about my job?'

Continue asking this second question making a list of your answers until you have all the possible answers. Then summarize the list and ask the question again. The thing *most* important to you may be so ingrained that you may not get to it until you have dug very deep indeed. You might list up to eight values, if not more.

In our example, you might get results, such as 'It's important that I am appreciated and valued at work', 'It's important that I am well paid' and 'It's important that my job has meaning – that it improves the world somehow.'

Step 2

Now, to find out what really is most important to you, take the value at the top of your list and compare it with each of the others in turn asking,

'Which is more important?' Be firm and don't let yourself off the hook. Do this for each value in the list. You will end up with with a hierarchy of values in relation to your chosen area.

Step 3

Now examine your top three values, one at a time, and form a view on whether what you are doing is expressing or violating these values. For example, if in your relationship with your son or daughter you have a high value around trust but you find yourself checking up on where they are and what time they are coming home then your behaviour is conflicting with your value. At this point you have a choice as to whether to keep the value and change the behaviour or vice versa. Other values will be driving some of your behaviour so it is important to remember that the object of this exercise is to gain clarity around your true values and the connection with your behaviour as this will help you to make decisions that serve you well. The intention is not to determine your number one value.

If your values are being violated what are you going to do about it? Can you change your behaviour to bring it into line with your values? Maybe one or more of your values is no longer valid and you have been hanging on to it through habit – where did it come from? Is it a value which works for you in some circumstances but not others? Can you change this value? Do you know someone with different values in this area? What would happen if you changed it? How would things be different for you? Asking these questions is the first step towards creating change.

Intrinsic values

So far we have looked at the values you have accumulated as a result of your life experiences. Underlying these are some deeper-rooted values which determine the way you approach life. They are called metaprogrammes – the source of your core motivation and behaviour patterns.

Intrinsic values are easily recognizable as programmes because they show themselves as patterns in what you say, how you say it and what you do. The key here is to decide not whether the behaviour is right or wrong but is it useful in the circumstances?

Think of these programmes on a continuum, with 0 and 10 representing the extremes. You might function at one point on the continuum at work, and at another in your personal life. There is no right or wrong – it is a question of whether it is useful in any given context. You will recognize yourself as we describe the extremes at each end of the continuum.

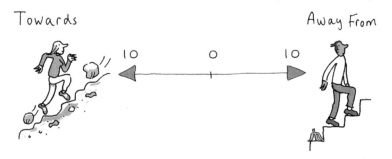

If you have a *towards* programme you are recognizable by your drive. You set goals easily and are frequently creating new goals for yourself. Sometimes you disregard the risks involved, and in the extreme may not complete one goal before beginning another.

- Advantages – forward-thinking, goal-orientated, positive energy and drive.

- Disadvantages – may get entangled by too many new initiatives at once; may be perceived as 'gung-ho'; has a tendency to leave things unfinished.

If you have an *away from* programme you focus on avoiding risks and making sure everything is safe before moving forward. You sometimes miss out on life and work experiences through fear of taking a risk. Typical behaviour includes being overinsured 'just in case', and when you are asked what you want you reply with a list of things you don't want. You hold back from getting involved in anything new until all concerns have been fully addressed. You put a high priority on all forms of security.

- Advantages – very good at assessing risks and recognizing what to avoid.

- Disadvantages – overly cautious with a tendency to focus on the downside; may appear negative and unwilling to try new experiences; makes choices based on avoidance rather than a desire for something new.

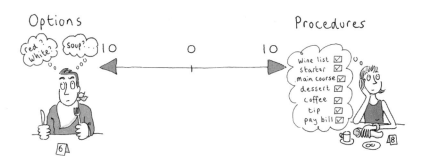

If you have an *options* programme you like to have choice in your life – considering different makes and models when buying a car, different areas when buying a house and the many varieties of food on offer when going out for a meal. In the extreme your behaviour can be perceived as procrastination, particularly to someone who values procedure. You have a tendency to keep going over and over choices, as if making a decision might cause regret later.

- Advantages – explores many options and provides people with choices; happy to test and break rules.

- Disadvantages – may procrastinate and avoid making decisions until forced to do so by circumstances; very good at reinventing the wheel.

In a procedures programme you have schemes to follow in order to be effective. You become confused and frustrated when faced with too many options. You write lists and tick things off as you go, and are very efficient at completing tasks which require an ordered sequence. You may, however, find it difficult to accept a new procedure, which is more than likely to have been written by an options-orientated person. In order to get involved in a creative thinking session you need a procedure detailing how to do it. You require structure and clear processes for getting things done.

- Advantages – very efficient; good with rule-based administration; will stick to agreed rules.

- Disadvantages – the procedure may become more important than the job to be done; at worst bureaucratic and blocking.

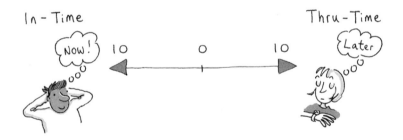

You are *in-time* if you live 'in the moment' not worrying about what comes next – whether you are going to be late for your next meeting or arriving late at a party, if indeed you get there at all. You give people your full attention because they are there with you now. You value each moment and are fully engaged with whatever you are doing at any time.

- Advantages – can concentrate on tasks; emotionally and mentally engaged in each and every experience.

- Disadvantages – frequently late and can give the impression of not being concerned about timekeeping; may get involved in too many things through attachment.

If you spend your time planning and making sure that you are not late for meetings, parties and any other engagements you have a *thru-time* pattern. This preoccupation with planning your next move or analyzing the last may prevent you from concentrating on the matter in hand. Your thinking is constantly flitting across past, present and future. You may appear to others to be disinterested.

- Advantages – good planner and timekeeper.

- Disadvantages – may give the impression of not being engaged in the current activity; being on time, and scheduling activities, can become more important than the activities themselves.

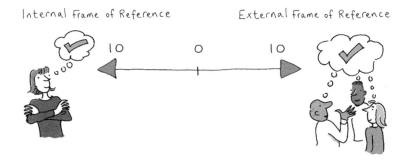

Internal Frame of Reference   External Frame of Reference

The simplest way to think about this pattern is in terms of how you measure yourself and how you evaluate situations. If you are *internally referenced* you instinctively know when you have done a good job and you will want to solve all your own problems. You rarely ask for advice from other people. You make decisions on your own judgements, feelings and opinions. You don't need reassurance from other people. In fact, if you are given such reassurance, thanks or appreciation you are likely to view it with suspicion. You will also know when you have done a job badly, and this again will be judged against your own criteria rather than external evidence. You can appear aloof and insular and possibly overconfident to an externally referenced person.

- Advantages – can stay motivated when there is little feedback or praise.

- Disadvantages – internal standards may override, and sometimes cancel out, external evidence; will disregard evidence, facts and sound advice from other people.

If you are *externally referenced* you measure yourself against the feedback from other people. You value this and will go out of your way to find it. To internally referenced people you can appear needy and lacking in self-sufficiency. When faced with a challenge you will seek facts, evidence, advice and opinions from other people and sources.

- Advantages – will make decisions based on concrete facts and evidence, or maybe just the 'feel good' factor so long as it comes from an external source; able to give excellent customer service and help to others.

- Disadvantages – will get stressed when there is a lack of external feedback. Needs frequent feedback on performance to make good progress; will be indecisive if there is a lack of feedback.

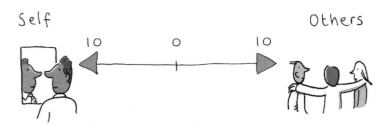

Who comes first – you or the team/family/group? If you have a *self* pattern you speak in terms of 'I' and 'What's in it for me?' You believe that people are capable of looking after themselves. You help yourself to coffee, push in front of traffic queues, take the last chocolate and put yourself first when making decisions.

- Advantages – looks after self and is very self-sufficient; avoids getting tangled up in other people's problems.

- Disadvantages – does not engender good team spirit and sometimes may be perceived as arrogant and/or uncaring.

With an *others* pattern you spend a lot of time making sure everyone is comfortable and happy and may neglect your own needs and wants. You serve other people coffee and put yourself last in the queue. You are a courteous driver and have a genuine concern for the well-being of others. Your day-to-day decisions are made taking account of other people, not wanting to cause them upset or discomfort.

- Advantages – good team player looking out for the needs of others; does well in caring professions.

- Disadvantages – personal well-being can suffer through putting other people first; can be perceived as unpredictable because many decisions are based on what others think and how they might react; considers the welfare of the team to be more important than getting the job done.

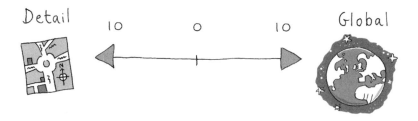

As a *detail* person you will be concerned about the specifics of a situation. Your conversations are likely to be long and drawn out to cover all the details. While focusing on detail you sometimes forget the overall purpose.

- Advantages – very comfortable working with details and excellent at spotting small mistakes; copes very well with large documents and small print.

- Disadvantages – can get bogged down in detail and work away happily, even though the purpose may have changed; may be perceived as pedantic or fastidious.

If you have a *global* pattern you look at situations from the bigger picture and speak in general terms avoiding detail. You move conversations onto different topics in preference to discussing details. You may have little to say about some topics, and may frequently need to be brought back to the point.

- Advantages – makes a good strategist or concept creator; can generate big ideas.

- Disadvantages – may appear to have the head in the clouds; may feel uncomfortable holding a detailed conversation; frustration with details may result in too many ideas and little execution.

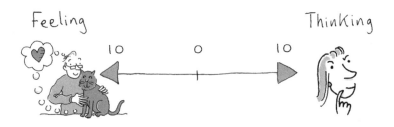

With a *feeling* pattern you react emotionally to a variety of situations and rely on your intuition or 'gut feeling' to make decisions. You are emotionally engaged with all life experiences.

- Advantages – takes people's feelings into account in making decisions.

- Disadvantages – can appear emotive; others may be wary of evoking an emotional response.

As someone with a *thinking* pattern you take a pragmatic and logical approach to situations while remaining emotionally detached.

- Advantages – decisions are made based on logic, fact and evaluation.

- Disadvantages – can appear to be cold and unfeeling; may not consider the feelings of others before speaking and acting.

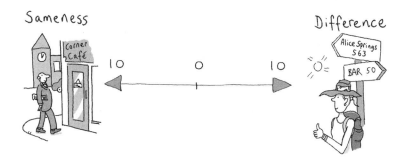

As someone with an extreme sameness pattern you will probably visit the same place on holiday every year, take the same route to work each day, sit at your favourite spot in your favourite restaurant eating the same food as you always do on the same night of the week. When approaching something new you will generate understanding by looking for similarities with previous experiences. Repetition doesn't bore you, it instils comfort and familiarity. You are likely to remain in the same job for many years.

- Advantages – can be relied on to complete repetitive activities successfully.

- Disadvantages – may be perceived as unadventurous by others; may not be willing to try new things even if they could be beneficial.

With an extreme difference pattern you are likely to be constantly on the lookout for new things to do or new ways of doing current things. You rarely go back to the same place twice, always wanting to try new foods in new restaurants and new locations for holidays. You get bored easily and may find yourself changing jobs frequently due to a need for difference.

- Advantages – happy to try out new ideas and concepts; gains many different life experiences.

- Disadvantages – sometimes creates change for the sake of creating change; doesn't understand the concept of 'if it works don't fix it'; lack of stability.

By now you will have an idea of your intrinsic values. With some you will already have the flexibility to be able to operate at either end of the continuum. If you operate mainly from one end, you might reap the benefits in some situations but you will also feel the effects of the disadvantages in others. If you can develop flexibility over all the programmes you will have the advantages with none of the disadvantages.

Mismatching of intrinsic values is a common cause of misunderstanding, stress and conflict in life. When people speak of a 'personality clash' it is invariably a mismatch of values or misunderstanding of metaprogrammes.

For example, many relationships break down because of a mismatch of the *in-time/thru-time* programme. As one partner is ready and waiting to set off to go out for a meal with friends the other is still chatting on the telephone showing no sense of urgency. The *thru-time* person feels devalued and frustrated while the *in-time* person wonders what all the fuss is about. It's the repetition and interplay of these patterns which eventually cause a relationship to break down.

Similarly you can bore a *global* thinker rigid if you give too much detail about your journey to work, or the state of your health, or what little Suzie got up to in the bath last night. Someone with a high value around choice is going to feel frustrated if asked to follow a five-step plan, and a person who is always late and unprepared will irritate someone with a high value around planning. Combinations of profiles can produce different behavioural patterns in different people. Mismatching of programmes in job profiles is a common cause of stress in the workplace.

These programmes are unconscious so when you become involved in activities which go against them you feel that uncomfortable tug. You may even say to yourself something like:

'Why am I always late for meetings?'

'Why is it that Sally and Paul always manage to book their holiday well in advance and I'm still messing around with the brochures when they are jetting off?'

'I hate my job but I'll stay because I'm not sure whether I would enjoy a new one.'

'Why do I never finish anything before I start something new?'

'I never seem to make up my mind to do anything.'

'It doesn't matter how hard I work, my manager never seems to appreciate me.'

Are your intrinsic values holding you back?

The examples above demonstrate conflicts of intrinsic values, each having advantages and disadvantages. They indicate a lack of flexibility due to being 'stuck' at one end of a continuum. Here's an exercise to help you to identify any patterns that may be the cause of conflict.

Identifying a conflict caused by an intrinsic value

Step 1

From the programme descriptions, choose those where you consider yourself to be predominantly at one end of the continuum. Write the name of the programmes below.

Programme: _____

Programme: _____

Programme: _____

▶

Step 2

Pick a situation where you have experienced conflict with another person, or frustration with a task or responsibility.

Situation: _____

Step 3

Consider the role you have been playing in this situation and ask yourself which of the programmes you identified in Step 1 are responsible for the conflict. Imagine how it might change if you were to function from the opposite end of the offending continuum. Take your time to think this through carefully. Acting so differently may feel awkward, but this is merely a sign that you have begun to develop your behavioural flexibility.

How you respond to experiences will depend on the nature of your values. If you once trusted someone and were let down there are a number of ways in which you could respond. You may decide never to trust anyone again, or you may decide that any future trust will have conditions attached. Alternatively you may retain your belief in trusting and hope that one day this person will also realize that. Each of these reactions has a very different underpinning value which results from the meaning you have accrued from your life experiences.

Adapting your intrinsic values to give you more choice

An awareness of your intrinsic values is very often enough to create change.

Kim has an *options* and *global* pattern. She experienced feelings of inadequacy when her partner, who had a *detail, procedures* pattern, was able to book the family holiday efficiently taking care of all the details. He would spend time studying brochures and by a process of elimination decide on the right one and book it, apparently without any feelings of stress. When Kim tried to do the same she became distracted and overwhelmed by all the different choices. Once she realized this she was able to relax, laugh at herself and allow her partner to do what he is good at.

Sometimes, however, awareness is not enough and circumstances may suggest that a change in behaviour might be beneficial.

Martin realized he had a strong *difference* pattern and every few months he would become bored with his job and seek a change. Realizing that this was not a recipe for success he decided to accommodate his difference pattern **within** his role, and social life, and still be able to progress successfully at work. When the tugs of familiarity occurred he could recognize them quickly and deal with them.

2 Don't believe everything you hear!

Your beliefs are connected to your values and are very personal. They form a significant part of the pattern in your personal kaleidoscope. If you value trust you are likely to hold beliefs such as:

- people can be trusted
- there is no need for rules
- people can manage their own schedules and productivity
- my children will come home when they say they will.

If you have a high value on mistrust you are likely to believe the opposite:

- only fools trust others
- people are out to get me
- I have to watch what you are doing because you can't be trusted
- I have to phone my children when its time for them to come home.

The beliefs expressed above probably came from experience – and it's amazing how little you need to form a belief. How many times does Johnny have to be late home from school before Mum develops a habit of reminding him to come straight home because she has formed the belief that 'Johnny is always late home from school'? How many times do you have to be ignored by someone for you to formulate the belief that they are uncaring or arrogant? We're not saying that all beliefs are wrong or inappropriate, rather to test if they are acting as a barrier, or a limitation. Once you have formed a belief it can become self-fulfilling in that others behave in a way that is expected of them. For example, if Johnny believes that Mum anticipates him being late then he will develop the habit. If you regularly tell Johnny that he is lazy, he will prove you right. Holding a limiting belief is like wearing blinkers – you see only what you expect to see and block out counter evidence. Because your beliefs are personal, you will defend them and seek evidence to justify them. This is fine if the belief is positive, such as 'Johnny has potential that is worth developing', but consider the consequences of believing 'Johnny will never make the grade'.

Are you being held back by limiting beliefs?

So who is turning the kaleidoscope of your mind? Who is imposing their limiting beliefs on you? The people around you will undoubtedly have a hand in making small turns, changing your beliefs and having an impact on your behaviour.

A mother and daughter attended the same training course. About to embark on a physical activity, the mother turned to her daughter and said, 'you'll never be able to do this, you aren't coordinated'. Fortunately the facilitator overheard the comment and the girl was asked to walk across the room. She did so elegantly proving that she was indeed coordinated. Imagine being continually told that you are not coordinated – what kind of limitation would this put on you? How long is the list of activities you would go out of your way to avoid?

Think back to your schooldays. How many things did you do poorly or drop out of because you believed you couldn't do them? Did your teachers, parents or peers reinforce or help you to create any limiting beliefs? Take a few moments to think of all the things you might be doing now if you hadn't carried these limiting beliefs to the present day.

At work how many people are being held back by the limiting beliefs of their manager? In our workshops we find an astonishingly high number. Many managers don't delegate, encourage, stretch or even recognize superb performance in their people. One reason for this is their belief in their own capability as a manager, another is their beliefs about the capabilities of others. Helping teams to develop positive beliefs and values about colleagues can dramatically change attitudes, which quickly cascade through the company with subsequent improvement in performance. If you can identify and change a limiting belief you can make huge strides forward.

A single belief represents just a small part of the kaleidoscope pattern and often forms part of a cluster of similar beliefs. In the extreme, a cluster of limiting beliefs can lead into a whole host of unpleasant areas including phobias, blaming others, anger and low self-esteem. Being in control of your own kaleidoscope is therefore key to your success. This simple demonstration created an awareness for the daughter that completely changed her beliefs about what coordination means. She went on to complete the exercise and learned to juggle three balls in under ten minutes.

Beliefs can be either limiting or empowering. Are yours serving you well? How can you recognize them and what can you do about them? Let's look at challenging limiting beliefs that may be hindering you.

A hard-working woman recently presented us with the belief 'you have to work to earn money'. It was attached to a value about having enough money for her family to be secure. It was also important for her to have an active social life and spend time with her family. However, she had developed the habit of working late and at weekends. She became increasingly unhappy. When she realized that the belief was causing stress she let go of it. She continued to enjoy her job as well as spending time going to concerts with friends and being with her family. Very quickly her new, and more powerful, belief became 'enjoying time with friends will give me the fulfilment I am seeking'. This attracted a whole new set of beliefs about what she was and wasn't going to do. The initial change to her work belief triggered a series of belief changes, much like a falling stack of cards.

How do you recognize a limiting belief?

This may seem like a simple change, but beliefs can be stubborn defying the most rigorous logic. First you need to know how to identify a limiting belief from what people say. A limiting belief is a simple statement that will usually begin with one of the following.

■ I can't . . .

■ People should . . .

■ They don't want . . .

■ Everyone/no one thinks . . .

Here are a few classic examples.

■ I can't maintain a long-term relationship.

■ People never listen to me.

■ He is easily distracted.

■ Learning a foreign language is difficult.

■ I'm no good at maths.

Here's a simple belief-change exercise.

Shaking unhelpful beliefs

Whenever you hear yourself making the kind of statement mentioned above use this exercise. There are three steps to changing an unhelpful belief.

Step 1

Shake its roots by challenging it. Answer the following questions.

■ Have I always believed this?

■ Where did this belief come from?

■ Is the belief still valid?

■ What evidence do I have to support the belief?

- Who do I know who holds an opposite belief?
- What evidence suggests that the belief is untrue?
- In what way is the belief absurd or ridiculous?

Step 2

Find an alternative, more empowering belief – brainstorm for beliefs that open up more possibilities. This is a matter of 'trying on' a variety of beliefs until you find one that fits. Make sure that your new belief is stated in the positive – for example, 'I can learn a foreign language and I am learning something new in each lesson'.

Step 3

Integrate the alternative belief. Imagine how things will be different and gauge how you feel about this change. Imagine yourself doing what you will be doing. Imagine having a conversation holding your new belief. Is this motivating you? Does it feel good? If necessary try on another belief and go through the same process. Then select the belief(s) that make you feel really good about yourself. Before finally committing to the new belief consider how it might affect other people.

Congratulate yourself for having taken control of your kaleidoscope. You have rid yourself of a limiting belief and created another that is infinitely more powerful. Even better is that over time this new way of thinking will become a habit and you will generate empowering beliefs naturally.

3 Think your way to feeling great

When you feel anxious, uncertain, confused, angry or frustrated you become tense and stressed. This will prevent you from accessing all your wonderful inner resources. Whatever situation you are in, if you are feeling any of these it is unlikely that you will perform to your full potential. Think of a time recently when you were feeling stressed and recall what was on your mind. Your thoughts were responsible for creating your feelings. Every thought you have results in a feeling, so the way to control your feelings is to control your thoughts. Test this out – sit quietly and think of a situation when you did something you didn't feel so good about. Notice what feelings come up. Now take a deep breath and think about a situation where you did something you felt really good about and again notice the feelings that come up.

You have just used your imagination to recall two experiences which resulted in very different feelings. You can use the connection between your imagination and your feelings to put you in control and give you choice about the way you feel. Your feelings have a direct impact on your capability, regardless of the situation.

It's the first thought that counts

Everything begins with a thought, and this thought will attract similar ones until you have a cluster of thoughts. This cluster becomes a pattern of thinking which forms a habit. The habit will be applied to many different scenarios. Scientists believe that your conscious mind is able to cope with only about seven pieces of information at any one time and can become overloaded very quickly. This means that if you fill your conscious mind with negative thought patterns that create negative feelings you have no room for anything else. By taking control you are exercising more choice over your conscious thinking and the more you do this the more you will build a reserve of unconscious patterns which work effectively for you.

The first step in taking control is to be aware of how thoughts are generated. When you think, you have an internal selection process – to absorb everything happening around you would overload your brain – so you select what you consider to be important and ignore the rest. For example, think about a conversation you had recently, or a television programme you watched – how much do you remember? Chances are you will be able to summarize the event and expand on the aspects of most interest to you, but you won't be able to recall every word. Your internal selection process has chosen what it wants to retain as a combination of images and sounds with the feelings you had at the time. Added to this will be some internal dialogue – in other words, what you have said to yourself about the situation.

This is how you represent your unique version of reality – through pictures, sounds, internal dialogue and feelings, and sometimes smell and taste. You capture your personal understanding of reality through a combination of your external senses and your inner thoughts, and it is this captured version that you use to make decisions and form judgements. This unique perspective of events is called your 'internal representation' or 'map of reality'.

Let's take a look at these components of your internal representation, beginning with the visual sense.

Working with your visual imagery

Bring to mind a pleasant memory and spend a few moments enjoying it. Capture the imagery – come back to the book when you are ready.

Describe the image you created? Was it clear? Was it in colour? Did it have a frame around it or did the edges fade away? Did it have depth?

Was there any movement? Was it bright, or dark and murky? How about the contrast and detail? How close was this image to you, and did you project it above or below the horizon? Could you see yourself in the image, or was the image all around you? Just as you can look at the visual details of a photograph or a movie, you can look at the details of the images which make up your thoughts. These details refer to the qualities of the image but not the image itself. The ability to imagine and change these qualities is unlimited. The number of different qualities you can work with in your mental imagery will be determined by the amount of practice you have had at doing so. Just as you intentionally imagined a pleasant experience, the very same process happens hundreds, if not thousands, of times each day to represent each thought you are having. Sometimes you may not be aware of your mental imagery, but it is there nonetheless, and you can use this to good effect.

Let's play around with your visual imagery a little and see how easy it is to change, or reprogramme, your thoughts and feelings.

Zap away bad feelings

It is quite easy to eliminate bad feelings for any situation where you would like to feel more in control, or be more confident. Perhaps the thought of facing a difficult situation with someone is causing you to feel frustrated, tense or low in confidence. At times like these, when you are emotionally stressed, you consume a great deal of energy making yourself feel bad – even though you don't enjoy feeling bad, it may be something over which you have had no control in the past. When you are feeling this way you have entered the realm of 'self-preservation'. As a result your ability to think rationally and make sound decisions is impaired. The goal then becomes one of survival, saving face, winning or seeking recognition. You only have to feel this way once or twice before a habit, or programme, is formed – and then you have a set pattern of thinking yourself into bad feelings. Eliminate the bad feelings with the following technique.

Zapping away bad feelings

Bring to mind a specific time when you were unhappy with the way you felt or behaved. Now focus on the image that comes to mind as you first access the memory. Now quickly send it zooming away into the distance – as it goes notice that it gets smaller and smaller until it disappears completely. It's just like the starship Enterprise whizzing off at warp factor 10 into deep space and, in a fraction of a second, disappearing completely from view in an instant. You can do the same thing with all your images of unpleasant experiences – just zap them off into deep space. As you do, notice how much better you feel.

Now exercise your ability to *choose* something *different* using the following technique.

Choosing to respond differently

As soon as you have zapped away the negative image using the previous technique, bring to mind a memory with positive feelings attached to it. It might be an experience where you were very confident, or where you were highly motivated to get a positive result. Now work on the image. Make sure it is colourful, big and bright. When you have intensified these qualities bring the image closer and imagine stepping into it. Take a few moments to absorb and enjoy the positive feelings generated by this effect.

Working with your internal audio

As well as making pictures in your mind you can replay conversations with other people, environmental sounds and music. Do you sometimes replay conversations, or anticipate a future event, and actually hear what people said or might say? This internal audio may or may not be accompanied by images. What about your internal dialogue? What do you find yourself saying over and over in your mind? Your internal voice is very powerful and has a direct influence on how you feel at any moment in time. A great deal of emotion is carried in your tone of voice – both spoken words and those you say to yourself. Here's something to think about – if you were to tape all your internal dialogue for one day and then play it back, would it motivate you?

You can explore and change the qualities of your internal audio in much the same way as you do with mental imagery. Use the following technique to change the way you feel when you think about a future event. It can be used in all kinds of situations when you want to feel a certain way. How do you want to feel when you wake up in the morning? When you get to work on Monday? When your partner does something that annoys you? How many different voices can you create for yourself?

Use your inner voice to change the way you feel

Think about an upcoming event that is important to you, and decide how you want to feel at this time. Now choose an actor or someone you know well with a voice tone that fits with the energy you want to have at this event. Imagine that the event is just about to start and have a conversation with yourself in the voice tone you have chosen. For example, you may want to feel confident and determined to get a result. You choose the voice of one of your heroes saying 'This is an important day for me. I will be asking some tough questions and expecting clear answers. I will be positive, focused and determined to get a result we can act upon.' Now say it again and turn up the volume. Adjust the tone and pace until you begin to feel confident and determined.

You can also turn the volume down when your internal dialogue gets carried away with itself. When you keep repeating negative dialogue over and over, telling yourself what a mess you made of this or that, or

▶

churning over a work problem when you are trying to sleep, simply turn the volume down and notice the words fading away into the distance until they have gone completely. You can also change negative voices into humorous voices like Bart Simpson or Mickey Mouse. Notice how easily the negative feelings disappear!

When you realize that you have control over your inner voice and associated sounds you can walk around with a symphony orchestra in your head and a host of film stars and cartoons at the ready should you require their services. Have fun.

Feeling fantastic

The feelings you have during a day are the result of how you have chosen to associate with your experiences. This is the emotional domain. The word used to describe these feelings is 'kinaesthetic'.

Your feelings are generated from imagined events as well as real experiences. If you have an argument with a partner or a disagreement with a shop assistant, the feelings you have will be part of a learned pattern of reacting to those circumstances. A memory consists of visual, auditory and kinaesthetic elements, and sometimes includes smells and tastes. Feelings result from thinking in a particular way – for example, a feeling of apprehension may be the result of creating dark murky images and internal dialogue warning you to be on the alert for an awkward or difficult situation. Imagine the feelings of another person in the same situation who is creating bright clear images with internal dialogue full of excitement.

You have the capacity for a wide range of feelings from excited highs to heavy lows – and, at worst, depression. There are many techniques to help you feel the way you want to feel. Some of them help you to change the feelings you have attached to negative memories, others give you a way of creating any feeling you want at any time.

Use your best experiences to feel great

The way we attach feelings to our thoughts is very haphazard. We allow people and circumstances to influence the way we feel. Once a thought has a feeling attached it becomes well and truly anchored, so that each time we recall the thought the exact same feeling will surface. For example, when you look at a photograph taken on a great holiday, the feelings you had at the time will return. When you answer the phone and hear the voice of someone you had a negative experience with, you will feel the same way as when the experience happened. Anchored feelings become embedded in your memory very easily. A classic anchor is when you have a bad encounter with a sales assistant and decide never to visit the store again. Whenever someone mentions the store name you relive the feelings you had at the time of your encounter, even though it may have taken place a long time ago.

The process of anchoring feelings to thoughts is an automatic feature of the unconscious mind. The result is called a 'state' – not just a state of mind, rather a state of mind and body since the way you think and feel causes the body to become either relaxed or tense. Now what if you could use this process to create great feelings, or states, whenever you wanted them? In other words, exercise choice over the feelings you anchor and the states you create. What if you could produce feelings of being courageous, confident, calm, decisive, optimistic, attentive, playful, empathetic, curious or focused? What if you could create a positive state for learning and being open-minded; for leadership, motherhood, fatherhood; for being dynamic or having abundant energy; for love, sensitivity? Well, you can with this very simple technique.

Anchoring states you want

Decide which state you would like to anchor. Choose one from the list above, or you may have some other specific state. For the purpose of this exercise we will call this 'state X'. Read through the exercise and commit

▶

it to memory – you will need to keep your attention focused internally throughout the process.

Preparing for the exercise

You are going to attach a state to a trigger point somewhere on your body, such as pinching your ear or squeezing your thumb. Choose something you are unlikely to do accidentally and that you can repeat with precision.

The procedure

1. Recall a time when you had a strong feeling of having state X, and keep thinking about that memory. Choose any context you like as long as the feeling of state X is very strong. If you can't think of one then put yourself into an imaginary situation where you are in a high state X. Pay attention to the qualities of your image and any sounds. You are going to use this internal representation to intensify the feeling of state X. It may help to close your eyes as you do this exercise.

2. Project the image in front of you above the horizon level. Make sure that you are looking at yourself in the image.

3. Put a frame around the image. Make it colourful and bright with high contrast. If sound is involved adjust an imaginary graphic equalizer so that it is across the full range of treble, middle and bass. Make it surround sound.

4. Intensify the colour, brightness, contrast and sound.

5. Slowly bring the image closer to you – notice how the frame eventually disappears until the image is so close that it has enveloped you and is all around you. As the feeling of state X approaches the peak of its intensity set your anchor by gently squeezing your thumb (or

pinching your ear or whichever anchor you chose). Release the anchor as soon as the sensation begins to diminish.

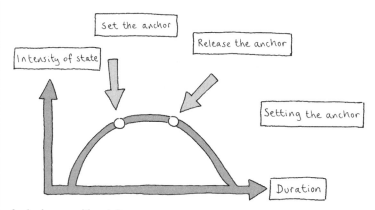

Anchoring a positive state

6. Now take a couple of deep breaths to change your state. Wait a few moments and then trigger, or fire your anchor! Enjoy the intensity of feeling X. Fire it a few times more to get used to it, and to strengthen it. Make sure you break your state by breathing deeply between each firing. Now you can use this anchor any time you want to have the feelings associated with state X.

You can test the anchor by future pacing. Think about a situation in the future where you will want state X. As you run through the scenario in your mind, fire your anchor. The key to successful anchoring is the intensity of feeling, the timing of setting the anchor and the precision in setting and firing the anchor.

In the same way as you can create a positive anchor, you can eliminate negative anchors. For example, you may have had a negative experience with someone in which you did not cope well. You may have had bad experiences at work that are still causing you to lose confidence or become frustrated. Your reaction in these situations creates a negative state which makes your inner resources inaccessible. Even though the incident might have happened some time ago you still carry the feelings associated with it and behave accordingly. Your behaviour reinforces your state and forms a strong habit, such that every time you find yourself in a similar situation the limiting behaviour is triggered. The following technique uses space and physical location to relieve these negative and stressful feelings. You needn't keep those bad feelings in your memory – you can collapse them and, if you wish, replace them with positive feelings.

Collapsing anchors

1. Mark two spaces on the floor about 6 feet apart.

2. Label one space with a negative sign, and the other with a positive sign.

3. Stand on the negative space and bring an unpleasant memory into your mind. Talk about the event for a minute or so and check how you feel as you recall the experience.

4. Take a couple of deep breaths and walk briskly over to the positive space bringing a pleasant memory into your mind – this must be more intense than the negative feeling. Talk about this experience for a minute or so paying attention to the images and sounds you use to recall the events. Intensify the qualities of colour, size, clarity, brightness and volume and bring the image close up. Bring the image closer and closer and notice how your feelings intensify. Hold this feeling for a few moments and then relax.

5. Staying on the positive space, talk again about the earlier unpleasant experience and notice how the negative feelings you had before have disappeared. You have collapsed the negative anchor.

Fixing your phobias

Phobias are exaggerated anchored responses to everyday situations – they can cause muscle tension, hyperventilation, perspiration and dizziness. When a phobic response is being experienced your internal dialogue and imagery will be predicting dire consequences. Phobias are irrational fears, as opposed to the rational fears caused by things that actually happen, such as the house being on fire. Because phobias are irrational they are relatively easy to overcome. NLP is very effective in fixing all kinds of phobias including fear of bridges, confined spaces, open spaces, flying, lifts, spiders, bees, birds, frogs and snakes. This even extends to phobias about wet hair in the shower plughole, oranges and bananas!

In our experience, many people try to hide their phobias and avoid situations where they may have to face their fear. This is because they perceive their problem as being ridiculous and try to avoid the embarrassment caused by their reaction. At a deep level this can have an adverse effect on self-esteem as a phobia is often thought of as a weakness. Underlying any phobia is a belief about what will happen in the situation causing the phobia. For example, when Paul was a teenager he choked on an orange. Over time he unconsciously anchored a negative response to this experience. Eventually this became a phobic reaction to oranges, to such an extent that he had to leave the room whenever someone began to peel an orange. He believed that if he ate an orange he would choke.

The test for whether a person has a phobia or not, as opposed to being merely very concerned, is that they will physically react very strongly to even the *thought* of their fear. Because it is the thought that produces the reaction it can be eliminated without having to relive the experience. If a phobia is affecting your enjoyment of life and/or your self-esteem, use the following technique – it has a very high success rate. We suggest that you familiarize yourself with the procedure before using it. This will enable you to complete the exercise without the distraction of referring to the notes.

Fast phobia fix

We are going to ask you to do a few things very quickly in your mind so that your phobia will never bother you again.

1. Imagine you are sitting in a cinema and on the screen there is a black and white still picture in which you see yourself just before your last experience of having the phobic response.

2. Now imagine that you are floating out of your body up to the projection room where you can see yourself sitting in the cinema – you can also see yourself in the still picture on the screen.

3. Turn the snapshot on the screen into a black and white movie and watch it until just after the unpleasant phobic experience. When you get to the end, stop it as a still. Now jump inside the picture and run it backwards in colour. Everything in the film will happen in reverse – people walking backwards, talking backwards and the scenery moving backwards.

4. This completes the exercise. Take a few deep breaths and test the results by thinking about what it was that you used to be phobic about.

Reframing

The exercises in this chapter have helped you to work with the emotions attached to your thinking and have given you access to your inner resources. There may be times when the *way* you are thinking is creating a barrier. You can change your perspective completely by reframing this kind of thinking in a number of ways. In the same way as placing a new frame around a picture can give it a whole new appearance, placing a new frame around your thoughts can give you a very different perspective.

Frank was 'at his wits' end' (his words) trying to get his youngest son Timmy to keep the house tidy. The relationship became strained as Frank continued to lay down the law. He often raised his voice and Timmy responded by retreating into silence and making himself scarce. The situation had been getting progressively worse and Timmy's performance at school was suffering. Frank explained that he was lost for a way to help Timmy 'get his act together'. Timmy was getting a hard time from his dad, and his falling academic standard was a direct result of stress. Frank was offered the following reframe.

'It appears you have been pushing Timmy to meet a certain standard of tidiness which is causing him a good deal of stress, and creating distance between you. Has it occurred to you that his untidiness may be a phase that kids of his age go through, and that it may be a sign that he's behaving normally? By letting him be a normal teenager, he might not be so stressed and be able to focus better on his schoolwork.'

In short, Frank was offered a reframe from 'my boy is untidy' to 'my boy is untidy which is normal behaviour for any teenager'. It helped Frank to realize that his behaviour towards Timmy had caused the breakdown in the relationship between them. He immediately stopped hounding him about being untidy and started to help him more with his schoolwork.

This type of reframe changes the meaning of the situation. Another type of reframe shifts the meaning between contexts. For example, a person who may be highly critical of other peoples' ideas might be perceived by his team as being difficult or negative. However, the presence of a critic on the team can be very useful when evaluating ideas resulting from a creative brainstorm. It's not that the behaviour of the critic is a problem, it's more a case of knowing how best to use this particular skill. This type of reframe puts the behaviour into a positive frame in another context.

A common cause of frustration between couples is demonstrated in this next example.

Fiona likes to be on time and is obsessive about dates, times, schedules and lists. Mike, Fiona's partner, is the exact opposite preferring to take a more relaxed and laid-back approach to life. Mike was feeling torn by wanting to please Fiona while being unable to rationalize the pressure he was feeling from her. After some coaching, Mike realized that Fiona's ability as an organizer was useful in many ways including remembering family birthdays, shopping, planning holidays and generally running the family very effectively. Having reframed his thinking in this way the pressure eased – it was attached to the way he had been thinking, and not to the circumstances.

Don't think **that,** think **this!**

Any reframe is simply saying 'don't think of it **that** way, think of it **this** way.' It's not that, it's this! You can apply simple reframes to all kinds of situations that are not working out as you would like. A problem can only exist in your mind – outside your mind there are only sets of circumstances. That you call a circumstance a problem is a factor of your thinking. One person's problem is another's source of motivation. So it really matters how you think about any situation you find yourself in, because there are consequences to your thinking.

The words **this** and **that** are used many times during the course of a day, but when used with tasks and people – for example **that** task or **this** person – they indicate whether the speaker is associated or dissociated with what they are referring to. Where there is a positive intention towards this task/person there is likely to be a positive mindset around it. When there is no positive intention towards **that** task/ person there is likely to be a negative mindset around it. Being dissociated with something is a source of procrastination. If you could choose not to get involved then there would be no issue. But when you *have* to get involved because it's your job to do so then you are forced to associate, and this is when negative feelings can take hold of your thinking. In situations of forced association it is useful to reframe your thinking and turn **that** into **this** with a positive intention.

There are four key principles involved.

1. You can be either *associated* (**this**) or *dissociated* (**that**) with tasks and people. When you are associated in a positive way you are emotionally connected and likely to achieve better results than when you have put distance between yourself and the task or person, thus becoming dissociated. Poor performance results from 'forced association' with a **that** – when you perform a **that** task without a clear positive intention you are forcing yourself to associate with it and the emotional connection is likely to be negative. This is a recipe for poor performance.

2. Having a conscious positive intention prepares the way for success – all your intentions are positive for you, even though it may not appear that way to other people. Your unconscious mind may be telling you not to go ahead with an unpleasant task because its positive intention is to keep you feeling good. Having a clear positive intention and looking for the good in the task allows you to take control of your success.

    Having no positive intention prepares the way for struggle – just as a clear positive intention clears the way for success, so not having one causes you to struggle. Your unconscious intention will be to feel better and look for ways which mean that you don't have to undertake an unpleasant task or meet someone who makes you feel uncomfortable. In doing so you cause yourself stress and discomfort.

3. When you exaggerate the absurdity in the way you are thinking about a situation you prepare the ground for change – you can find absurdity in almost anything and use it to create change. An example demonstrating this follows in the next section.

4. Changing **that** to **this** is primarily a matter of focusing on what is good and having a positive intention – the concept of yin and yang demonstrates that to achieve balance and flow in life everything

must contain an element of its opposite. Hot will contain elements of cold, good will contain elements of bad and vice versa. So every **that** must contain an element of **this**. Unfortunately while you are focusing on **that** you are oblivious to the **this**, which is undoubtedly present. Your results will be more successful if you choose to stay focused on **this** and allow it to develop and grow.

There can be any number of reasons why you consider something or someone as a **that**, for example:

- activities you don't enjoy and don't look forward to
- work that you don't feel fully competent to complete to a satisfactory standard
- someone or something you have negative beliefs about
- activities that conflict with a personal value
- someone you find difficult or frustrating to be with.

Using absurdity to create a change of thinking

You can find absurdity in just about anything. Consider the statement 'I have to have dinner on the table by 6 pm every day'. This implies that all the family members will be hungry and ready to eat at exactly the same time every day. The likelihood of this being the case is remote, and therefore the statement is absurd.

This technique takes the absurdity in your thinking and exaggerates it. In doing so your situation becomes so ridiculous that you will want to change your view and reframe it because it is too painful to continue thinking in the old way.

Peter was a project manager who was a real stickler for detail and procedure. He had been given responsibility for a major project involving Simon. Simon became more and more anxious whenever he thought about the project. Peter and Simon clashed from the outset. Simon didn't know how to deal with Peter when he insisted on introducing details that Simon believed were unnecessary at the meetings. This began to affect his ability to contribute rationally. He would sneer and make derogatory comments about Peter's style of management in front of the project team. When questioned about the situation Simon replied 'he needs to learn a lesson if he's going to get on – I'll teach him don't you worry'. He was offered the following reframe.

> 'So Simon, it seems you want to go on feeling bad about this relationship, don't you? You are going to continue to snipe at Peter and have everyone else laughing and sniggering at you behind your back. You don't even mind that they perceive you to be behaving like a child. The project will suffer and your emotional energy will be tied up in creating negative feelings towards Peter so you will have very little left for creativity around the project. However, you won't mind that because teaching Peter a lesson is so much more important to you than building good relationships and getting the project completed successfully. Your antagonistic behaviour will serve you well when you find yourself not being invited onto the team for future projects. You may even find yourself without a role at all and that's OK because the most important thing here is to make Peter look silly, isn't it?'

This technique may appear a little harsh, but with the right person it could be the most effective tool to use. In this case Simon is the type to allow his ego to get in the way, and so the technique had to be stronger than his overinflated ego. What Simon received was a reframe from 'Peter needs to be taught a lesson' to 'my career is more important than the way I feel about Peter'. This caused sufficient pain to Simon's ego for him to let go of the need to teach Peter a lesson, and make positive adjustments to his thinking and his behaviour.

Focus on a positive intention

The absurdity technique may do the trick for some people (we hope you tried it out on your own situation with state X), and sometimes you may need a little more positive encouragement. However negatively you view a situation or a person, there is always some good to be found.

Michelle was having a problem with her flatmate who seemed to be interfering in her life. She took it to mean that her flatmate didn't trust her to make her own decisions about boyfriends. Michelle began to mistrust her own judgement and became withdrawn, refusing invitations to nights out. When questioned she said that her flatmate didn't want her to have a good time and was jealous of her boyfriends. This frame of thinking caused a deep rift in the friendship. Michelle was offered the following reframe.

'Michelle, could it be that your flatmate cares about you and doesn't want to see you get hurt? Maybe she has had a painful relationship and doesn't want you to experience the same pain. Perhaps your focusing on the perceived jealousy is keeping you from noticing ways in which she really does care. However it may seem to you, the reality could be very different. If she did care for you, what is it that she does that will tell you this?'

Michelle decided to look for evidence that her flatmate really did care about her well-being. She discovered lots of small things she did for her that had previously gone unnoticed. The relationship improved and they healed the rift. The point at which this situation turned around was when Michelle flipped her **that** mindset to **this** mindset and created a positive intention to find the good in her flatmate.

Flipping a that to a this

1. Think of a task you really don't enjoy doing which causes you to procrastinate or one which you do very quickly to get it out of the way. Whichever, it causes you bad feelings, and possibly to perform lower than your usual standard.

2. Create a conscious positive intention for completing the task and begin to focus on this intention.

3. Either use the absurdity technique described above or begin to develop the positive aspects of the task, or both. How absurd is it that you have been thinking of the task in that way? Keep looking for the good and release your mind from the negative aspects of the task.

Thinking in **this** way will allow your mind to be creative and to come up with solutions and ideas rather than becoming stressed by the bad feelings associated with **that**-type thinking.

4 Organize your thinking for successful results

So far we have focused on how one thought leads to another and how your thinking determines your behaviour. It's your behaviour that has an impact on the people around you, and it's your behaviour that people respond to. Your attitude of mind is an important factor in forming your behaviour – if you have an aggressive attitude your behaviour will take on aggressive qualities; if you have an attitude of superiority your body language will send that message to others; a relaxed attitude will result in a relaxed posture.

So your attitude directly affects your behaviour and consists of a collection of experiences generalized into a set of values and a complex web of beliefs. In *Changing Belief Systems with NLP*, Robert Dilts developed a universal model to explain how this works. You can use it to organize your thinking for successful results in any context. You consider each of five levels of thinking in relation to any specific purpose:

1. identity
2. values and beliefs
3. capability
4. behaviour
5. environment.

Awareness of these levels will make it easy to choose the most effective NLP technique for the change you wish to make. The key to using this model begins with a clearly defined purpose.

Is your purpose crystal clear?

In all situations you have an intention. Often this is unconscious – you engage with other people or undertake tasks without first thinking what you intend to achieve. For example, what is your intention for having a particular conversation with your partner? Is it to inform, to gain support, to satisfy your need to be heard, to seek attention, or something else? What is your intention for undertaking a part-time job or choosing a new career? Is it to leave behind a tedious or stressful job, to do something you have aspired to for some time, to increase your income, or to have flexible working hours? If your intention is unclear then you run the risk of behaving in a way that will sabotage your best efforts and leave you feeling dissatisfied. A classic example of this is where someone is feeling bad about their life in some way and decides to move to a different city or country for a fresh start. At a deep level the intention is to remove the bad feelings, which have grown over time. What often happens is that the new life follows exactly the same pattern of events as the previous one.

Having a clear sense of purpose will give you conscious choice about how you approach situations. It will bring your deepest intentions to the surface and will determine the role you play in the pursuit of your purpose. Having clarified your purpose the next step is to organize your thinking within each of the five levels of alignment.

1 What role are you playing?

In life you play many different work, family and societal roles. You may split your time between being a parent, sibling, provider, chairperson, technician, leader, carer or any number of combinations of roles. What's important here is not the *label* for your role, but how you define it. This has an impact on your results. The manager who defines her role as taskmaster and organizer will get a very different response from her team than the manager who defines her role as people developer. Children of parents who define their role as protectors will grow up very differently from children whose parents define their role as nurturers. The teacher with a role of disciplinarian and controller will get very different results from another who defines her role as challenger and learning facilitator.

The role you define in the pursuit of your purpose will interact with your values and beliefs, which determine what you pay attention to and what you ignore.

2 What values and beliefs do you hold?

To be a nurturing parent you will probably have strong values around providing opportunities for life experiences for your children. As a manager who believes in getting the best out of people you will have strong values around trust and the potential of your team. As a teacher creating a positive learning environment you will have values around discovery, exploration and creativity.

These values will be supported by any number of beliefs. The nature of a belief is to cause you to focus on your values and to prove the belief to be true. So whatever you believe to be true you will seek evidence to prove it and ignore evidence to the contrary. This is why it is so important to make sure that your beliefs are empowering you to achieve the results you desire. For example, a teacher with the belief that a child has a learning difficulty will continue to reinforce the difficulty. On the other hand a teacher with the belief that the child has potential, and that the challenge is to find a way to release it, will undoubtedly get better results.

3 Are you limiting your true capability?

Your values and beliefs have a direct impact on your capability. Quite simply, if you believe that you can then you will find a way of doing so. If you believe that you can't then you won't bother to look for a way. Empowering beliefs unlock capability and limiting beliefs act as a barrier. Limiting beliefs stop you from putting effort into things. It's like the kaleidoscope being stuck with the same pattern – you have the power to change it but refrain from doing so because you are either unaware or unsure of the consequences. Eventually the pattern becomes dull and loses its excitement. Once you believe it's not possible to change it then you will find every excuse to make this true. It is very common for people to develop illness as an excuse for continuing to believe that they can't achieve something. You only have to look around to find many examples of people who have achieved great things through the power of their belief. Values and beliefs work together – if you value something enough you will generate a belief that it is possible to achieve and put your energy into finding a way.

Sally opted out of a language exercise saying she was no good at English. She explained how her English teacher had encouraged her to pursue a career with numbers because her English was so poor. She followed this advice, took a job as a junior accountant and disliked it intensely. She left after three years to work as a shop assistant from where her career developed. On being quizzed on her current role she revealed that she had been promoted into the customer services team and now writes letters for the department – and that she really enjoys it. Sally also receives regular praise for the quality and creative nature of her letters. However, despite this praise, she still maintained the belief that she was no good at English, and developed the habit of withdrawing from any activities based on language. The acceptance of her teacher's belief limited Sally's natural ability in this area for many years.

4 Is your behaviour aligned with your thinking?

Your behaviour is a result of the way you have organized your thinking at each of the three levels above. Once Sally was able to change her belief about her capability in English it opened up a whole new range of activities for her. She began writing short stories and articles, and even attempted some poetry. Some of your behaviours will be working well for you, others not. Once behaviour becomes a habit it is almost unrecognizable by you – until someone points it out.

A group of elderly couples were walking arm-in-arm through a hotel lobby to dinner. One lady was limping and carefully holding onto a man's arm. As she limped across the room she suddenly realized she had left her glass of wine at the bar and took off with a determined stride to retrieve it. She had forgotten to limp – the limp was not in her leg but in her mind.

So which parts of your behaviour are no longer of use to you? What tugs are you feeling? What would happen if you gave your kaleidoscope a small twist?

5 Are you having an impact on your environment?

The way you organize your thinking at the four levels above will determine the impact you have on your physical environment. Limiting beliefs and an unclear purpose create stress. The blame for stress is often placed on external factors in the environment. This moves the focus away from self and in doing so takes away the power of influence. With empowering beliefs and a strong sense of purpose you are more likely to take responsibility for changing your environment. Even unconsciously you are more likely to have a positive impact. Often you may believe that the environment is causing you some stress and feel emotionally tugged. The stronger the limiting beliefs about your capability then the more likely it is that you will recognize what is wrong in the world, yet do nothing positive to create change. People who change things believe that they can.

The first step to taking control is to identify the level at which a tug is taking place.

Are you aligned with your purpose?

Sometimes a change of behaviour does not follow a change of thinking. Have you ever been in a position where you have done something you didn't want to do? Perhaps you did it to please someone and then felt you had done yourself a disservice. Or maybe you made a decision to lead a healthier lifestyle and take up running or yoga, but when the time came to attend a class or go to the gym you let yourself down and reverted to your regular unhealthy habit. It's at times like these that you feel the instinctive tug of misalignment.

In NLP this state of misalignment resulting in a behaviour that doesn't fit with the other levels is called 'incongruence'. Deep inside you want to act a certain way, but when the time comes you resist the inner urge and maybe tell yourself 'not this time, maybe next time'. This is incongruence; not something success thrives on. Success requires congruence, and this means an alignment of all the levels from purpose down through to the behaviour. Only then can you affect your environment in the way you really want. This is the process of building self-confidence – knowing that you have executed a change of mind and acted accordingly. Being able to recognize when you are being incongruent is the first step in making your desired change happen.

The feeling of incongruence doesn't have to stem from a major life realization – it can happen during the course of a business meeting, or in a conversation with a partner. So whatever you are doing, it pays to be able to recognize feelings of incongruence.

When you take a close look at the times when you are being successful, chances are you are also feeling happy and confident. Sure, you can imagine all kinds of bad things happening if you choose to, but when you are engaged in the act of doing something superbly well is when you will be at your happiest. There is a saying, 'if you have to ask yourself if you are happy then you are probably not'. Happiness is a state of mind, and you arrive at it through being congruent in your actions.

Happy people attract happy people

In the same way that similar thoughts congregate in clusters, so do people. If you feel depressed you will attract depressed people and upbeat people will avoid you. If you gain the skills to help people to improve their lives, those who need you will find you. If you decide to be unhappy, you will be. Life works in this way – it will bring you what you express with your whole being. Cynical people keep each other company and strengthen their cynical attitude. The key message here is 'what energy are you giving off, and who and what are you attracting?' Your feelings of incongruence are likely to transmit signals that other people will perceive as confusing and unpredictable. As a consequence they may judge you as being unreliable.

You hear people referring to others as being smug, with a chip on their shoulder, arrogant, brash, stand-offish, stuck up, cold fish. These are all interpretations of the way a person is communicating. It may be true, but as soon as you have interpreted a person's behaviour you have also chosen to relate to them with that judgement in your mind. The real truth lies beneath the behaviour in the kaleidoscope of their thinking. What is being picked up is a misalignment between levels – the result of the unconscious tugs referred to earlier. The key is to develop 'curiosity' about what is causing a person to behave in such a way, rather than to interpret the behaviour you see. This way you are less likely to fall into the trap of acting from a misinterpretation, and more likely to begin to understand the person and communicate with them effectively.

In our work we meet all kinds of people who come to us because they feel stuck with some aspect of their life. We have worked with managers who are not making the progress they want with their team, life coaches who are struggling to make ends meet, couples who have lost the excitement in their lives, directors who are petrified at the thought of giving a presentation to the board, professionals who are snowed under with tasks getting stressed and losing sleep, workers who are not meeting their employer's expectations of performance, people with obsessions, phobias, stress, anger, frustration, apathy and all kinds of behaviour patterns that are causing problems. We meet people from all walks of life who are limiting their potential to succeed and be brilliant in all kinds of situations. The one thing they have in common is a feeling of incongruence when they think about the conflict they are living with. What they discover is how one frustration or problem is related to others such as weight loss or gain, smoking, cluttered thinking, frequent illness, low self-esteem, being able to feel and patterns of broken relationships.

When you feel under stress through personal difficulties your mind has a wonderful capacity to put your problems behind a veil. This allows you to have some stability and maintain the status quo of your life. However, passion and energy also become masked behind the veil. Even though you can create a smokescreen for your thinking, your body is not easily deceived.

You can fool your mind but not your body

Your mind and body are part of the same energy system and interact with each other in response to external stimuli. When you are having a tough day, and your mind is working flat out to meet deadlines, stress accumulates in your body – for example you might become tense and your breathing erratic. Your body will react to whatever changes your mind goes through, and vice versa.

Your body gives signals to other people. So even though you may be able to create a smokescreen and veil your problems in your mind, others will intuitively know that something is incongruent. The only way to deal with this is to remove the veil of your thinking and create a change. One of the people Bandler and Grinder modelled in the early days of creating NLP was Virginia Satir, a highly effective family therapist. Virginia achieved very quick results by using a unique way of helping individual family members become aware of their incongruent behaviour. The behaviours she identified in *People Making* are not exclusive to dysfunctional families. You only need to look around to see them everywhere.

Satir categories

Virginia had four behaviour categories that were responsible for many family conflicts, and one that can be used for resolving conflict and bringing people together.

Distracter

Distracters seek attention to compensate for their feelings of loneliness or inadequacy. The positive intention behind their behaviour is to protect them from facing up to things. Distracting behaviour includes removing a hair from your jacket lapel while you are talking, sabotaging a conversation by making a joke, interrupting a conversation, frequently changing the subject. There are many other types of distracting behaviour that people use to deflect attention from a subject that may be reminding them of their feelings of loneliness and inadequacy.

Placater

The placater is out to please – talking in an ingratiating way, never disagreeing and always seeking approval. Feelings of an inability to cope alone create a martyr or 'yes man' (or woman!) A placater is often the first person to accept the blame when things go wrong.

Blamer

Blamers find fault – never accepting responsibility themselves, always blaming someone or something else. They feel unsuccessful and lonely. They often suffer from high blood pressure and come across as aggressive and tyrannical. They will tell you what is wrong with things and whose fault it is, and in doing so become powerless to do anything about it. By blaming external factors they have absolved themselves of responsibility.

Computer

Computer-like behaviour is very correct and proper but displaying no feeling. The voice is dry and monotone and the body often very still and precise in its movements, which are minimal, masking a feeling of vulnerability.

Leveller

The only place to be – levellers have few threats to their self-esteem. Words, voice tone, body movements and facial expressions all give the same message. Levellers apologize for an action, not for existing. They have no need to blame, be subservient, retreat into computer behaviour or to be constantly on the move. They are great communicators and have the ability to build bridges in relationships, heal impasses and build self-esteem.

How does a leveller think and behave?

The leveller response is a real-time congruent response. All the other responses are the result of negative internal feelings causing words and actions to be incongruent. It is very easy, under pressure, to respond to a situation with 'it's not my fault' or 'I'm sorry, it's my fault again', or to laugh inappropriately or show no emotion at all. None of these behaviours allow you to seek out rational solutions. The leveller response is the most effective behaviour for solving problems creatively.

Levellers:

- look for solutions
- have a conscious positive intention behind everything they do
- hold strong positive beliefs about themselves and others
- operate from strong personal values
- store positive mind images
- have flexibility of behaviour when communicating with others
- establish rapport before trying to influence.

All these attributes can be learnt through NLP using the techniques in this book.

5 Using rapport to build successful relationships

We all need people in our lives – to love us and to be loved, to buy from and sell to, to coach and be coached, to teach and to learn from, and to enjoy life with. The results of your interactions with each individual will be determined by your ability to get on with them, to be influenced by them and to influence their thinking and behaviour. Whatever you do, your ability to influence others in all kinds of ways is important if you want to be more than a passive onlooker. Whether you are parenting, buying, selling, managing, leading, coaching, mentoring, relaxing or having fun, your degree of success in all these areas will come down to your ability to influence, and this requires skill in building rapport quickly.

Think about times when other people have tried to influence you. Perhaps you have experienced a pushy sales assistant or a prescriptive boss or an overbearing partner. How did you feel at the time? Think of a time when you were enticed by a sales assistant – what did he or she do that enticed you? Would you warm to someone whom you felt had no respect for you? Would you feel comfortable with a person who makes no attempt to understand your needs? Probably not. Strong rapport is required to hold up a strong relationship – much like strong foundations will hold up a tall building.

Developing your ability to build rapport can help build confidence and contribute towards a more rewarding lifestyle with friends, colleagues and family. Rapport often develops naturally and you probably don't notice when it's happening. We expect you already have rapport with many people, but there will be occasions when a person who is important to your success is not on your wavelength, and you will need to work at building the relationship.

The role of respect in building rapport

In order to build rapport you must first decide to respect the other person's perspective. How can you build rapport with someone if your outcome is uncertain or you don't feel confident in your role in that situation, or you have a conflict of values? If you attempt to fake rapport you will get caught out – people pick up your true motives and feelings through your body language and tone of voice. So if you are insincere it will show. If you want to create rapport with someone you must do it from a position of respect and a genuine need to understand them and seek win–win outcomes. When you feel congruent with your outcomes, identity, values and beliefs then your behaviour will follow naturally.

Using what you do naturally – matching and mirroring

Have you ever watched two people deep in conversation? If they are both engaged in the exchange they will unconsciously copy each other's body postures, movements, voice tone, pace and breathing. Sometimes they do it exactly, other times they mirror each other. It's like dancing to a rhythm. You can use this as the foundation for building rapport with anyone you choose – in NLP it is called matching and mirroring.

Basically, people like people who are like them, so a sure way of building rapport with others is to be like them. You can build relationships and influence a wider variety of people by becoming consciously aware of what you do when you naturally have rapport. When rapport has been lost you can take decisive action to rebuild it.

Using your body to build rapport

There is a common misconception about body language – you can interpret what it means. If you base your approach to people on your interpretation of their body language you will get it wrong much of the time. Interpretation will not get you very far. It is more useful to use what you notice about a person's body language in the matching and mirroring process. So crossed arms doesn't necessarily mean that somebody is closed, they could just be feeling comfortable that way. If you also fold your arms you will be joining them in their 'dance' and they will feel comfortable with you. However, knowing how people have a tendency to interpret body language and often get it wrong, you need to be aware of your own as others are likely to be making judgements about you from your posture, gestures and tone of voice.

Matching and mirroring body language is a highly effective method of creating rapport. At first it may seem a little wooden but as you practice it and learn to do it naturally no one notices. It is an unconscious process. To be proficient at it requires you to overcome any apprehensions you may have. It's like learning anything – practice makes it easier to do. Things that you can usefully match include:

- physiology – body posture, position, movement, gestures (when you are talking), breathing
- voice – tone, speed, volume, pitch, timbre, rhythm
- language – key words
- values – (personal and intrinsic) what people hold as being true and important
- experience – common interests.

Matching and mirroring takes place at the behavioural level. Think back to a time when you felt awkward building rapport and it just wasn't working, no matter what you tried. What was going on for you? Was it anything to do with the mirroring and matching or was it more to do with what was going on inside your head? Using the above list to match and mirror, how would you create rapport with a two-year-old child? How about a teenager? A pensioner? A particular person you want to influence at work?

How to match and mirror to create rapport

1. Think of someone you have not seen eye-to-eye with – where a better relationship would be good for you both. Imagine meeting this person.

2. Notice their posture and body language, and match or mirror it. You don't need total precision when matching. Are the arms folded? Is the breathing fast, slow, shallow or deep? Are the legs crossed? Notice the gestures used and use the same gestures when you are speaking. Raise or lower your voice tone and pace to match. Above all be curious about what they have to say, and acknowledge that you are listening. When you speak use the same words as they do wherever possible rather than substituting your own preferred words – for example, don't use 'shop' for their 'store'. This may seem unnatural, but it works. It is giving the other person a very strong message that you are a lot like them.

Time taken creating and building rapport will pay dividends in the influencing process. Be open and willing to be influenced by another person's perspectives. If you attempt to gain rapport and yet show no interest in understanding the other person you are unlikely to succeed. Lasting rapport requires sincerity and receptivity – you should really understand the other person's unique perspectives of how things are, and not push yours onto them.

Pacing and leading

Having created rapport you now have a foundation for influencing. Generally speaking, a person is unlikely to accept your views, opinions and goals unless they can form some attachment to them. Just telling a person what you want is not a smart option. First make sure you have strong rapport, and then gently lead the person towards your thinking and create as much attachment for them as you can.

Pacing is the ongoing process of matching the other person's unique perception, thus strengthening rapport. The same applies in group meetings and presentations where you might begin by pacing common views or experiences. Once you have gained a good level of rapport by pacing, begin to lead and influence the other person or group. Check if the other person is willing to follow you by changing your physiology and noticing what happens – if you have rapport they will follow you. If rapport is lost during leading, revert to pacing and regain rapport before continuing to lead to a desired outcome. The general view in NLP is that you need twice as much pacing as leading.

Taking the lead with your ideas

When you introduce a new topic to a conversation, unless the topic is popular you risk breaking rapport. Why should anyone want to listen to what you have to say? Most people attempt to introduce their idea into a conversation and justify it – we all like to defend and protect what we consider to be important. A smarter way of getting your idea accepted is to connect it with the idea already held by the other person. You are then able to make a smooth transition to your topic. Minds like to be led to new ideas.

People communicate using different size chunks of information across a continuum, with detail and global at the extremities. You can use this concept to pace and lead elegantly.

Here's a simple example of how information falls into chunk sizes. Just take the word 'tree' which is part of a wood, which is vegetation, which is part of the ecosystem. So we have 'chunked up' from tree to ecosystem. You can just as easily 'chunk down' from tree to oak to branch and to leaves. You can also move in a lateral direction from any level – for example, a lateral move from the word oak would give us types of tree such as birch, fir, pine, coconut, etc. There are only three directions you can take during a conversation – up, down and lateral.

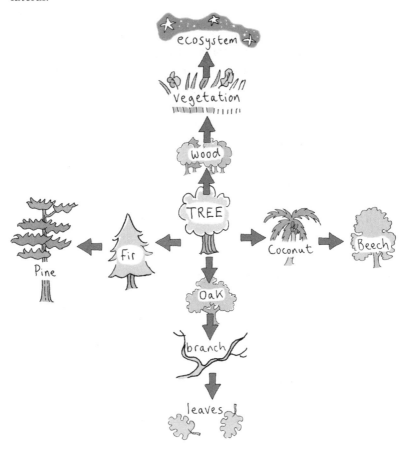

Here's how you might use chunking to gain financial support for a project.

You arrive at your manager's desk to find him deep in conversation about the latest cricket test match. You are not going to be very popular and probably won't get a result if you begin talking about money immediately. You need to find a way to lead him from 'test match' to 'financial support'.

In this example there are seven levels but in reality a conversation can range over any number of levels.

1. Corporate finance

2. Sponsorship   **Finance**

3. Professional sport

4. Test match   International football, golf, tennis, rugby

5. Teams and clubs   Australia, England, West Indies, Pakistan

6. Players   Umpires, spectators, organizers

7. Batsman   Bowler, fielder, wicketkeeper

From 'test match' you may choose to chunk up to professional sport, sponsorship and corporate finance, or down to specific teams, the players and the roles they play. Here is how the conversation might go – notice how Kate joins the conversation at level 4 and takes it to level 2, from where she can naturally introduce her idea for sponsorship.

> Peter (manager) – Did you see any of the test cricket yesterday Joe? (level 4)
>
> Joe – Yes, isn't X playing well? (level 6)
>
> Peter – I love test cricket. I find it relaxing and exciting at the same time. (level 4)
>
> Kate (arriving) – I saw the match yesterday too. My partner is a cricket addict (level 4). In fact he is a sports fanatic full stop. (level 4)
>
> Peter – Oh really. What other sports does he like? (level 4)
>
> Kate – He is a member of the Y football club (level 5) and gets to see quite a few matches from the sponsor's lounge because he works for the Z software company. (level 5) They did really well last year out of a new product they introduced and sponsoring Y is giving them loads of publicity. (level 2) They can't seem to do any wrong at the moment.
>
> Peter – Perhaps we should think about sponsoring a club? (level 1)
>
> Kate – Perhaps when we have got this new marketing campaign off the ground it will give us the publicity we need to be able to approach a club. (level 1) I've actually got the figures here for you to look at Peter. (level 2)

By working the levels in this way you will be able to raise the chunk size to a level where you can 'cross over' to your topic. In this case the cross over was reached at level 2 when Peter joined the conversation about sponsorship – it was a simple step to introduce finance. What you are doing in a strategy like this is joining the other person's value and staying with it linking their value in a subtle way with your topic. It's about facilitating a smooth transition across topics.

Here are some more examples.

- Getting your young son from 'PlayStation' to 'room tidying':

    You – What level are you on with your new game?

    Son – Level 6.

    You – What do you have to do to get to level 7?

    Son – Shoot all the aliens in the way.

    You – Wow that'll tidy up all those aliens won't it? How many aliens are there in your bedroom?

    Son – Don't know.

    You – Shall we count them?

    Son – OK.

    You – Now what shall we do with them to clear them out of the way?

- Getting your partner from 'football' to 'holidays':

    You – What's the score?

    Partner – 2–1 to United.

    You – It looks really sunny where they are playing. Is it in this country?

    Partner – No it's in Barcelona.

    You – Wouldn't you rather be there watching the match in all that glorious sunshine?

    Partner – Of course I would.

    You – Why don't we book a holiday in Spain and soak up some of that lovely sun?

- Getting your ageing parent from 'what's wrong with me' to 'let's go out somewhere':

    Parent – I feel really ill today. I really don't know what's wrong with me.

You – Really? What's been happening?

Parent – I keep getting dizzy spells when I get up out of my chair.

You – Dizzy spells? What are they like?

Parent – It's like having little stars in front of my eyes. They soon go away but it frightens me when it's happening.

You – Stars are really pretty. Why don't you try and capture them for a moment before they disappear? In fact today I am going to take you to see lots of stars including the biggest of them all, your granddaughter. We are going to the children's pantomime at the school. Come on, let's get ready.

You can have a lot of fun with pacing and leading as well as avoiding potentially confrontational situations. You will be surprised how easy it is to connect things in this way once you have practised.

Fine-tune your senses for feedback

The communication process is greatly enhanced if you can learn to recognize the state changes discussed in the previous chapter in other people as well as yourself. This means sharpening up your senses so that you can spot changes in yourself and in others that usually go unnoticed. In NLP this is called 'sensory acuity'. Without good sensory acuity any techniques you learn will be very limited indeed. How can you have any influence if you are unable to read the way people are communicating and feeling? You may passionately explain to someone how your master plan is brilliant, but if they think otherwise, and you miss their signals of disbelief, then you have only convinced yourself!

To influence anyone you need your senses tuned in to certain physiological signs that indicate whether they are with you or not. If you miss the unconscious signals people transmit through their body language and tone of voice then you are ignorant of most of the message they are conveying. What you want to do is to realize when a person's state has changed, and whether the state they are in is useful for the outcome you have in mind. If you are selling, you want your customer to be in a 'buying' state. If you are giving a presentation, you want your audience to be in a 'receptive' state. When we run workshops we make sure that we pace and lead our participants from whatever state they are in when they arrive to a 'curious to learn' state before getting into the first session. We can only do this if we have the sensory acuity to identify the initial states.

It makes sense to prepare yourself, and others, before engaging in a matter involving communication, or even when just relaxing. Surprisingly few people intentionally prepare their state for what they want to achieve. It is easy to end up with an inappropriate state for all kinds of activities – for example, going to seminars with a 'you can't teach me anything' state or 'another boring seminar' state; going to work with a 'I hate Mondays' state or 'I'm not looking forward to the meeting' state; arriving home after a long day's work with a 'please don't ask me for anything' state or a 'kids are making too much noise' state.

Here are some of the outward signs to look for when trying to 'spot' a state:

■ voice characteristics (tone, speed, timbre, volume, flow)

■ body posture

■ tension in certain parts of the body

■ breathing pattern

■ lip size

■ pupil size

■ lines on the face

■ skin colour.

Assessing these external indicators of internal states is called 'calibrating' a state. Think of it as taking a reading of a person's state.

Noticing and recording states for future reference

When you meet a person who tells you that they are feeling frustrated, this is the time to calibrate their state by assessing all the aspects of their physiology listed above. This will be their 'frustrated' state and you are unlikely to connect with your topic while this state exists. If you ever have to deal with this person again you will know when they are frustrated. If they screw up their face and squeeze their fists and grind their teeth you can begin to pace and lead them into a more receptive state.

Some people will not be easy to calibrate, typically those who like to keep their emotions to themselves. This is where your skills of sensory acuity and calibration will be fully tested. Look carefully for changing aspects of their physiology – maybe a very slight change in posture or lip size, for example. The signs will be there as the body always responds to a change of state.

To develop your sensory acuity you will need to practise calibrating the physiology of people as they change between states. Avoid trying to interpret what any state means. If you say 'Jack looks depressed' you may be correct, but then again you really don't know unless Jack previously told you he was depressed and his physiology at that time was the same as it is now. You can only truly interpret what a state means when the person has given you evidence that describes it.

Give people time to think

In any form of communication, people need time to think about what they are listening to and observing. They want to process information as it is received. While doing so they have to stop listening – in NLP the term used for this is 'downtime'. Having the sensory acuity to notice when a person is processing in downtime is fundamental to rapport building, pacing and leading and ultimately to effective communication. For example, during a conversation if a person has their eyes open and directed your way does it mean that they are looking at you and listening? They could be, but then again if the eyes are glazed over or focused somewhere in the distance their vision is likely to be in downtime thinking of something else. The senses of sight and hearing can be directed either inward or outward. When you are 'in your head' running images, conversations and other sounds that make up your thoughts, you will not be taking in any information regardless of where your eyes are looking. In order to be fully alert to what is going on around you your senses must be focused outward. When you are in conversation with another person you know if they are listening to you by their eye movements – roving eyes or a distant focus tell you that there are other thoughts inside their head.

Reading eye patterns for useful information

There are many aspects of a person's physiology that give clues to how they are thinking or feeling. One of the biggest giveaways is the movement of the eyes. Once you know certain movements you can determine how a person is accessing information, and you can use this knowledge to influence them.

The eyes are considered to be windows to the soul. They also indicate the way a person is thinking. Because the eyes are hard-wired to both sides of the brain they move in accord with the thinking process. So, unless you are a gifted mind-reader, you will not be able to tell *what* a person is thinking, yet with a little practice you will be able to tell *how* a person is thinking. You know that a thought can consist of visual, auditory and kinaesthetic information, and this is revealed by the position of the eyes. Just think for a moment how you can use this information with people you want to influence. If you could tell whether a person is thinking in pictures, sounds or feelings would you be able to communicate more effectively with them? Would it give you an angle on influencing them? The danger is that you miss the signals and totally mismatch their mode of communication – for example, using a 'feeling mode' with someone who is processing in a 'visual mode'. This is a common and frequent cause of miscommunication between people and, at worst, can create conflict. Depending on which direction the eyes are looking you can pick up the mode in which the person is thinking as shown in the diagrams that follow.

Characteristics of communication modes

The following descriptions are valid for a right-handed person. Some left-handed people may be configured the opposite way around. While you read the descriptions keep in mind that we use all the modes of communication – however, some people may rely on one dominant mode and use the other modes with far less frequency and clarity. Whichever mode is used most often, that will be the mode in which you are able to make the most distinctions.

Visual thinking mode

Upwards at any angle above the horizon is where the eyes go when you are accessing images. Up to the left indicates the recall of a visual memory and up to the right indicates a constructed image. Flicking from up-left to up-right and back again indicates that both recall and construct are taking place. People who use the visual mode frequently in their communication often speak quickly and in a high pitch as they synchronize their voice with the images flashing through their mind. This process affects the breathing because when you speak quickly there isn't time to take in air all the way down to the lower abdomen. So you will notice the upper chest rising and falling.

Visual recall

Visual construct

In conversation the visual communicator will have a tendency to choose visual words, such as:

'Can you *see* what I mean?'
'I'll *paint* you a *picture*.'
'It's *bright* and *clear*.'
'Let's *zoom in* on this.'

Tessa functioned at such a fast rate in the visual mode that she had 'forgotten' how to feel. She could see the solution to problems so quickly in her mind that she didn't stop to think about how she or anyone else felt about them. People had trouble keeping up with her, and consequently her ability to communicate effectively was impaired. Over time she had become severely stressed and was having medical attention for conditions that appeared to exist only in her mind. Upon recognizing this, and after some practice she was able to reconnect with her feelings. She went on to make some major changes in her life and is now a much happier, healthier person.

Auditory thinking mode

A lateral-left movement indicates a remembered sound such as a conversation or piece of music. Lateral-right indicates a constructed sound or conversation. People who use the auditory mode frequently in their communication tend to have voices that are pleasant to listen to. They are likely to breathe from the mid-chest area.

Auditory recall

In conversation the auditory communicator will have a tendency to choose auditory words, such as:

'I *hear* what you say.'
'That *rings* a bell.'
'It *sounds* OK to me.'
'It's *music* to my ears.'

Auditory Construct

Paula lived with her elderly mother and was becoming increasingly frustrated about the amount of time her mother spent watching soaps on the television. Paula functioned mainly through the auditory channel and couldn't understand the need for such visual stimulation. However, Paula would go about her daily jobs with her personal stereo plugged in listening to 'The Archers'. Both were interested in soaps through different channels and with her newfound awareness Paula was able to be a great deal more tolerant of her mother.

Internal dialogue thinking mode

When the eyes are down-left it indicates an inner conversation. We all have a voice that we use to talk with ourselves in our thinking, or to run habitual loops of dialogue. There is no characteristic breathing pattern with this mode, but it is common for someone in deep conversation with themselves to put a hand on the side of their face, or to stroke their chin.

Internal dialogue

This is the classic pose of 'the thinker'. You my even see the jaw moving as if words are being mimed.

Betty believed she had a learning difficulty as she struggled to remember anything from lessons she attended. She had always thought this was due to a lack of intelligence and poor memory. During a training course she learned how her internal dialogue was really to blame. Each time the trainer asked Betty a question he noticed, from her eye positions, how she had been engaged with her own dialogue and therefore had not been listening to what was going on in the sessions. On realizing this she made a conscious effort to stay tuned in to the trainer and over time managed to tame her inner dialogue.

Kinaesthetic thinking mode

Kinaesthetic

Eyes down-right indicates someone immersed in a feeling. They are likely to be breathing from the lower abdomen area and will be speaking slowly, with gaps between the words. Sometimes the gaps will be long. The gaps are needed to allow time for feelings to form before committing a word or phrase to speech – it must feel right before it is said. The voice will be low-pitched.

In conversation, the kinaesthetic communicator will have a tendency to choose feeling words, such as:

> 'This just *feels* right.'
> 'Let's *run* with this idea for a while.'
> 'You had better *get your skates on.*'
> 'We're in for a *bumpy ride* over the next week or so.'
> 'Let's keep in *touch.*'
> 'I *get the hang* of this now.'

Graham used his feelings to communicate almost exclusively. During conversations he would take such a long time to form an answer that the person he was talking to would move the conversation on before he could finish a sentence. This led Graham to believe that people weren't interested in what he had to say. As a consequence he developed the habit of tailing-off his sentences before coming to the end. This reinforced his belief because people not only had to wait for him to reply but couldn't hear the full sentence when he did. Once Graham realized this he was able to finish his sentences with the same emphasis as he started with and to change his belief about people not being interested in him.

Knowing how a person is communicating is very useful if you want to 'get on the same wavelength' and make your communication as effortless and effective as possible.

Underlying these techniques is the responsibility that *you* have for the communication process. Do not expect others to fit in with your style. Your flexibility to adapt will give you greater powers of influence. So if you are asking someone a question using the visual mode, 'How do you see this panning out?', and the reply 'I don't see anything' comes back, it could be that you have mismatched the communication mode. If, using your sensory acuity, you notice the other person using the kinaesthetic mode, you could then modify your question to fit – for example, 'How does this feel to you as it begins to unfold?'

By modifying just a small aspect of your communication you can have a significant influence on people. It's not so much the content of what you are saying that makes the connection, but the way you say it. Applying what you have learned about the visual, auditory and kinaesthetic modes of communication can have a big impact on how others respond to you.

6 The impact of words

You learned in the previous chapter how to pace and lead using the concept of information chunk size, and how words are an effective tool for creating change. Your language is just the superficial expression of the structure of your experience, in which lies your kaleidoscope of values and beliefs. In the same way that your thinking becomes habitual and forms unconscious patterns, so does your language. Your memory bank of language consists of stock phrases that you use repeatedly. These reinforce your thinking and a cycle is established. Is your language working for you or against you?

How to use high-level language for positive results

High-level language, or large-sized chunks of information, is vague. Consider the statement, 'kids nowadays don't care'. It is vague because it omits the detail of 'which kids', 'which days', 'how they show they don't care' and 'what they don't care about'. A statement like this will have been formed as a result of the speaker applying their personal values and beliefs to their experience. The danger is that the speaker will now seek further evidence to defend the statement and ignore anything to the contrary. Compare this with the same pattern used in a positive way, for example 'kids today are so creative'. Its vagueness begs the same questions, but the consequences are far more uplifting and empowering.

Both these statements demonstrate the three ways in which the mind selects and attaches meaning to experiences for storing in the memory. The first is through *generalizing*, as in 'kids'. The second is *deleting*, as in 'how specifically they don't care' or in 'what way they are creative'. The third way is *distorting*, as in 'don't care' and 'so creative' – this is being distorted to fit the perception of the speaker, in other words what he has chosen to believe.

Milton Erickson was a highly effective and unconventional therapist. His methods were modelled by the originators of NLP (*Patterns of the Hypnotic Techniques of Milton H Erickson, MD* by Richard Bandler and John Grinder). Milton used vague language to help people change the way they think. The language patterns he used became known as 'artfully vague' language. He used the patterns to help people change the way they represent their experiences internally, rather than giving direct advice on what to do. Your personal perception of events is called your 'map of reality' and no two persons' maps are alike.

Milton realized that his clients *wanted* to change, but making them defensive would not help. So he agreed with whatever his client presented as their map of reality, no matter how absurd it sounded. He then used language to make it easy for the client to create their own change.

A sales executive wanted to improve his results, but was hesitant when talking to new prospects. The root of the hesitancy was an experience where a visit to a new prospect didn't go well. The prospect ignored him and 'made him feel small' (his words). His memory of this event brought up the emotion of 'feeling small' which became a barrier to gaining new clients. After coaching, he changed his perception of the negative experience and this allowed him to be confident about future visits to new prospects. As a result his new client conversion rate increased significantly. During the coaching he was questioned and offered statements that agreed with the way he was thinking. The manner in which the statements were delivered caused him to realize the absurdity of what he was doing to himself. One of the statements that created a big shift for him was, '*Wow! Isn't it incredible how you instinctively know that all new prospects are waiting for you to call on them so that they can make you feel small?*' This statement agreed with his map of reality, while emphasizing the absurdity of it. So there was nothing to defend or disagree with.

Think how often you use limiting language to yourself to determine what you can and can't do. Next time you hear yourself saying that you can't do something you would like to do, just listen to your reasoning and ask yourself where such 'beliefs' – because that's what they are – have come from.

Here are some language patterns to look out for. If you find yourself using them in a positive way then generate more. The examples here demonstrate patterns being used in a limiting way and include questions that help to create positive change.

Generalization

This is where the speaker has taken a particular experience and applied it to a multitude of other situations.

'You can't run a family and work full-time'

- Questions – What can you do? What stops you? What tells you that? Who can't? Do you know anyone who does? How many hours and days are you thinking of? What if you could?
- Words to listen for – can't, unable, not possible.

'Children need discipline'

- Questions – Need? Which children? Discipline in what way? What else do they need? Who says?
- Words to listen for – need, must, have to, got to, necessary, requirement.

'Nobody loves me'

- Questions – Nobody? Is there one person who does/doesn't? What tells you that? How are you measuring love? Do you love anyone?
- Words to listen for – everybody, nobody, anyone, every, always, never.

Deletion

This is where detail has been deleted as the speaker chooses what to focus on. Here are some examples.

'He's a failure'

- Questions – How did he fail exactly? What did he fail at? Who says so? Has he failed at everything he's done? Is there nothing he has succeeded at? Has he not succeeded at drawing your attention? What else is he succeeding with?
- Words to listen for – instances where a verb has been turned into a noun such as 'failing at' becomes 'failure' or 'he is performing' becomes 'his performance' or 'he is succeeding' becomes 'his success'.

'Her children are not very bright'

- Questions – Compared to whom? What standard/who are you measuring them against? Bright in what way?
- Words to listen for – those which require an opposite such as good, bad, cold, hot, bright, dull, sincere, insincere, happy, sad, rich, poor.

'She rejected me'

- Questions – What did she do that you are calling rejection?
- Words to listen for – verbs which require clarification.

'They were left to fend for themselves'

- Questions – Who are they? What do you mean by fend?
- Words to listen for – non-specific references to people/things such as they, people, computers, children.

Distortion

'He never buys me flowers so he doesn't love me'

- Questions – In what way does him not buying you flowers mean that he doesn't love you? So what ways does he show that he loves you?

- Words/patterns to listen for – statements that don't 'add up', where a conclusion stated in the second part is based on the meaning attached in the first part.

'My children are driving me crazy'

- Questions – What specifically are they doing to cause you to feel crazy? What are your children doing when you choose to go crazy?

- Words/phrases to listen for – statements in which one thing causes another.

'I know you don't want to support my initiative'

- Questions – How do you know? What tells you that? You can read my mind?

- Words/phrases to listen for – statements which include conjecture and suggest mind-reading.

'Families should stick together through all life's challenges'

- Questions – Who said that? Who are you quoting?

- Words/phrases to listen for – statements lacking reference to the author.

NLP calls the above 'metamodel' questions because they bring into awareness a higher level (meta) meaning of words. They bring into conscious awareness the deep-rooted patterns of meaning that have been created from values and beliefs. All too often, negative vague language becomes part of the programming used in everyday life. You have seen how easy it is to develop beliefs that have a major impact on the way you behave. Your language is greatly influenced by your beliefs and associated values. Artfully vague language patterns are positive and offer alternative choices in such a way that the individual is empowered to make whatever changes will help to get better-quality results. Think of the metamodel as an antidote to limiting vague language. It seeks out clarity by getting to the specifics of an experience. It does this by questioning the generalizations, deletions and distortions.

When we break down language in this way it's easy to see just how our thought patterns become demotivating and limiting, not only for ourselves but for the people around us.

More insight as to the way we use language can be gauged from the way we use the past, present and future tenses. You will often hear people say things like:

'I will never be able to do that.'
'I can't go under water.'
'I'm not a team player.'
'I don't seem able to hold down a job.'
'I can't run for more than 10 minutes.'
'My manager and I don't see eye to eye.'
'I'm no good at numbers.'
'If I tried that I'd certainly fail.'

Note that all these statements are in the present tense – as a human being you have an amazing capacity to carry past experiences with you. Sometimes this is enjoyable, as when you recall pleasant memories and plan your future based on memorable experiences. But when you apply the present tense to negative experiences it can limit your potential. Your memories can be like old clothes – they become unfashionable or worn out but you can't bear to throw them away. So they hang in the wardrobe taking up space and preventing your other clothes from looking fresh and smart.

The problem with the makers of the statements above is that the desire to change is overshadowed by the strength of belief they carry. By changing the tense of statements you can start to gently shake the intensity of the limiting belief. For example:

'I will never be able to do that' *becomes* 'Up to now I have not been able to achieve this.' (Notice also the subtle change of 'that' to 'this' suggesting association rather than dissociation, in turn implying desire and ownership.)

'I can't go under water' *becomes* 'Until now I have not felt comfortable going under water.'

'I'm not a team player' *becomes* 'My experience of working in teams to date has not been enjoyable.'

'I don't seem able to hold down a job' *becomes* 'In the past I have had some challenges settling into a job.'

'I can't run for more than 10 minutes' *becomes* 'I have run for up to 10 minutes.'

'My manager and I don't see eye to eye' *becomes* 'My manager and I have had one or two differences in the past.'

'I'm no good at numbers' *becomes* 'I have had a challenge or two with arithmetic.'

'If I tried that I'd certainly fail' becomes 'I have never tried this before but I am willing to have a go.'

The last statement is interesting in that it is not even based on past experience. It predicts what will happen and prevents the speaker from trying something new.

Putting the statements into the past tense suggests that there is a *possibility* that things can change. To create a real change in behaviour you have to work on designing the future. For this to happen there has to be real desire. With a real desire to change you can add the future intention. For example, a person with a real desire to build a relationship with his manager might say:

'In the past my manager and I have had our differences but I am going to make a real effort to listen and understand his point of view'.

The person having difficulty with arithmetic but with a real desire to keep their household accounts in order might say:

'In the past I have had some challenges with arithmetic but I am going to take some lessons and practise adding up so that I can keep my household accounts in order.'

We encourage you to listen closely to the words people say, and to your own internal dialogue and to challenge it where appropriate using the metamodel questions.

Using metaphors to create change

Further insight to thinking can be gained by recognizing metaphors in language. They are very effective when pacing and leading other people.

Some people have a way of using metaphors to describe their map of reality. These patterns have become part of everyday language. Here are some common examples:

- It's like watching grass grow
- She was like a bull in a china shop
- This is the Rolls-Royce edition
- It's like walking through treacle
- We need to ride the storm.

Metaphors like these are a manifestation of a map of reality. Identifying with a person's metaphor can create instant rapport. You can pace and lead someone effectively and elegantly by picking up on their metaphors without even knowing the true content of their meaning. Here is an example from a conversation between David and Ben.

> Ben – It's like the car is running, the wheels are going round but we're not going anywhere.
> David – Really! That must mean the engine's working very hard.
> Ben – You're right – it is.
> David – Then that must be putting a lot of strain on the engine.
> Ben – You are absolutely right – it's like there is so much detail and I can't join up the dots.
> David – Which dots?
> Ben – The dots of my aspiration.
> David – What do the dots look like?
> Ben – I don't know – actually there aren't any.

In this conversation David first joined Ben in his metaphor. He then led him from a state of frustration to a realization that his stress was of his own making. Ben didn't know where his stress was coming from. By developing the metaphor he became aware that the cause of his stress was an aspiration without a plan.

Persuading with elegance

It is easy to let words pass as the urgency to 'have your say' takes over. Every word can have an impact. Are your words having the impact you want?

The aspects of language covered in this chapter give you alternative choices in the way you communicate. If you put them all together and practise you will be able to influence and persuade elegantly. Because language has such an immediate impact you will find that your words will increase your personal power in such areas as:

- getting your ideas across
- coaching others
- working with groups
- presenting in public
- teaching
- negotiating
- parenting
- working through personal problems.

Above all it will give you more confidence and positive energy in all areas of your life.

7 Debug the programmes you don't want

You have now covered all the main components that are involved in the way you communicate with yourself, and with others. The diagram below shows how NLP puts it all together. Through generalizing, deleting and distorting information you create a state, which drives your behaviour. This is how your programmes are formed.

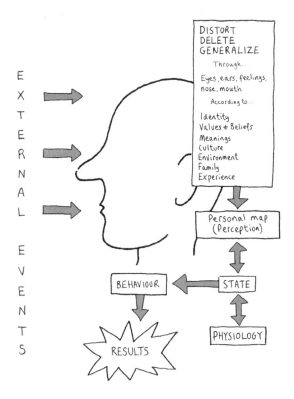

You have a programme for everything you do – motivating yourself, procrastinating, negotiating, getting tired, buying things – and for all the things you would rather not do but continue with because you have formed a strong habit. This programming consists of a sequence of thoughts and behaviour which are triggered by a stimulus. In NLP this is called a 'strategy' for achieving an outcome. If you have ever tried to break a habit and failed then it is more than likely that you were unaware of either the trigger or the unconscious parts of the strategy. Once you know about all the components of the strategy you can do any number of things, including:

■ changing it for something more useful

■ copying an effective strategy from someone else

■ designing a new one from scratch.

Dennis was very careful with his money. When he made a decision to buy something he would follow a set strategy, which went something like this:

■ Visualize myself using it (internal visual)

■ Do I really need it? (internal dialogue)

■ If yes, research the model/type/make/price (internal visual)

■ Who shall I ask for an opinion? (internal dialogue based on external reference metaprogramme)

■ Ask Jack and Bob (external auditory)

■ Yes, that feels right (kinaesthetic)

■ Where shall I buy it from? (internal dialogue)

■ Consider internet/shop/mail order (internal visual)

■ Yes, that feels right (kinaesthetic)

■ Buy!

Compare this with Beverley's strategy of –

- That would look great on me (external visual)
- Try it on (external kinaesthetic)
- Looks good, feels good (external visual and external kinaesthetic)
- Buy!

Some people who are good at spelling use a strategy consisting of visual pictures of the letters placed in the correct order, usually brightly coloured. A common reason why some people are not good spellers is the strategy they use. Poor spellers often try to spell by pronouncing words with their internal dialogue. Anyone can be a good speller – you only have to learn an effective strategy using visuals of words and not just what they sound like.

Ineffective strategies prevent people from achieving so many things. How well do you manage your finances? What about the presentations you have given? How well do you communicate with people at work? Are you a good cook? What about the way you make decisions? Can you maintain positive and fruitful relationships? Whatever aspect of your life you feel you want to improve you can bet there is a strategy holding you back, either creating inertia or producing undesirable results. The key is in knowing the beginning and end of each strategy, so that you can change it.

Eliciting a strategy

When you elicit a strategy you will discover values, beliefs and metaprogrammes plus a sequence of thoughts and behaviour.

Eliciting a strategy

Choose something you do that you would rather not do, or something you would like to improve upon – for example motivating yourself, stopping procrastinating, improving your decision making, giving up smoking.

Find the TRIGGER

- How do you know when to do this?
- What lets you know you are ready to do this?
- What do you do as you are preparing to . . .?
- What steps do you go through?
- What happens next?
- Then what happens?
- How do you know when you have succeeded?
- How do you test whether or not you have succeeded?
- What lets you know if you have not yet succeeded?

Check the strategy

When you have elicited the complete strategy repeat it back to check for anything missing. If you want to change it, the place to do this is at the trigger point. The object is not to remove the original strategy but to create an alternative choice, as the strategy may be useful in other contexts.

Norman wanted to stop smoking. He could manage without a cigarette most of the time but found the urge irresistible when he had something to celebrate. At these times his strategy included a visual of his hero on top of a mountain smoking a cigarette. This resulted in a strong belief that 'all successful people smoke' hence his need to smoke when he felt successful. Once he realized this he changed his belief to 'no matter how successful you are, smart people don't smoke'. He was then able to modify his strategy at the trigger point, removing the cigarette from his visual of his hero. As a consequence he lost the urge to smoke.

Creating a new strategy

1. Think of a strategy you would like to have, for example:
   - getting out of bed with a spring in your step
   - losing weight
   - keeping fit
   - arriving home after work feeling energetic
   - getting to sleep
   - doing your accounts
   - paying the bills
   - helping the children with their homework
   - improving your sports performance.

2. Create strong VALUES and rock solid BELIEFS, stated in the positive, about the desire to have the strategy – for example, 'When I have this strategy I will be able to do/have . . .' or 'I really want this strategy because . . .' and 'I can be/do . . . whenever I choose to be/do'

▶

3. Decide on the trigger for your strategy. For example, if you want to lose weight it could begin whenever the thought of food crosses your mind or whenever it is time to prepare a meal or sit at the table.

4. Create a powerful series of images of you succeeding with the strategy. Break it down step by step making each image big, bright and colourful. Keep the images dissociated and use strong, empowering internal dialogue.

5. Mentally practise your new strategy in slow motion as many times as it takes to programme your thinking.

6. Test the strategy by imagining a time in the future when you will want to use it. Run it through in your mind.

8   Fantastic outcomes

Earlier we introduced the five levels of alignment. We suggested that for you to live a happy and fulfilled life all the levels have to be aligned. What actually happens is that no matter how well aligned you think you are, life has ways of enticing you to become misaligned. The decisions you make every day will either pull you closer to being aligned, or push you further away. Sometimes you can have all your levels lined up but still feel a tug. This can happen if your outcome is not clearly defined. In NLP goal setting is about setting 'well-formed outcomes'. For example, if you are about to make a telephone call to a new partner, or apply for a new job or promotion, have you thought through the possible outcomes? What is your outcome for attending the sales meeting next week? What is your outcome for spending time with your children? What is your outcome for having that night out with your friends? What is your outcome for your new business idea, for joining the squash club or for taking up t'ai chi or yoga?

Once you have established a clear outcome you can decide what role you will play, be able to establish your values and beliefs around the situation, develop your capabilities, adjust your behaviour and have a positive impact on your surroundings.

Do I need a purpose or an outcome?

Think of 'purpose' as being a higher level than identity, more about the essence of who you are than a description of your role. It is considered by some to be close to your spirituality.

Colin described his role as 'a life coach working with people to facilitate positive personal change'. He described his purpose as 'to help people realize their true potential'. As he goes about his work as a life coach Colin keeps this purpose at the forefront of his mind. However, his outcome for each session will depend on the individual needs of his client.

A strong sense of purpose provides the energy to move forward with certainty and confidence; outcomes focus on having clarity for your desired results in specific situations.

Outcomes differ from goals in that a goal usually takes the form of a short statement about what you want to achieve. An outcome considers other consequences of the effort applied to achieving the goal. When you merely state a goal then that is what you measure. By setting outcomes there is so much more you can achieve.

Tim set a goal to increase new account sales by 15% by the end of the quarter. His outcomes, as a result of having achieved the increase, were 'for his team to feel good about their contribution; for the new clients to be happy with the service; for potential for further added-value sales; for the team to have learned more about selling and influencing.'

Making sure your outcomes are well formed

The acronym PRIEST provides a framework with which you can determine the strength and validity of any outcome to ensure that it is well formed.

P is for positively stated

A feature of the human mind is its inability to process a negative. Consider the following instruction, 'whatever you do, do NOT think about a pink elephant.' Oh! Too late, you thought about one didn't you? We know you did because you *have* to think of the thing you are not supposed to think about! Beware of your capacity to 'get what you focus on'. If your main focus is on what you *don't want* you may end up getting it! Make sure that your outcomes are clearly stated in the positive – in other words what you *do* want, not what you *don't* want (a pink elephant).

R is for resources

This includes internal as well as external resources. Do you have the courage, confidence, staying power, commitment, determination and other internal resources you may need to succeed? If not there are NLP techniques you can use to acquire them. What external resources will you need – finance, people, knowledge?

I is for initiated and maintained by self

Is the achievement of this outcome totally in your control or does it depend on something outside your control? You may want to adjust your outcome if you are not fully in control. Even if you involve other people to help you, make sure you keep hold of the responsibility for your choices, even when things don't go according to plan.

E is for ecology

Have you considered the consequences of achieving your outcome? What are the likely impacts on other people and other aspects of your life? Are they acceptable to you? This is known as an 'ecology check'.

S is for sensory evidence

What sensory evidence will tell you that you have successfully achieved your outcomes? What will you hear? What will you see and how will you feel? Take some time to imagine how things will be in the future having achieved what you set out to achieve. How will you know you have been successful?

T is for time

What timescale are you working to? How long will it take you to achieve all the outcomes attached to your goal? If you write out your goals it is very easy to miss something. The following exercise uses space and visualization to help you set a realistic timescale and to check how well formed your outcomes really are.

Visualize your success

Find a quiet space where you can visualize the journey of achievement. Mark a space on the floor to represent 'now'. From this space walk to a point on the floor a particular distance away to represent the time you think it will take you to achieve your outcomes. Stand on this point and look back to 'now'. Spend some time feeling what it's like to have achieved all your outcomes.

Next, walk a little further into the future and turn around. Look back to 'now' again and visualize what you did to achieve your outcomes. Make sure your internal language is in the past tense. Once your mind has grasped the idea that you have already succeeded, visualizing what you *did* as opposed to what you *have to do* is a much more creative, insightful and far less stressful process. It's very powerful, and great fun too.

Linda likes to look after people and entertain. Her outcome for a night out was to make sure that Joy enjoyed her birthday after a period of illness (positively stated). She booked Joy's favourite restaurant, made sure all the guests were happy to contribute to the event, took responsibility (initiated by self) for making sure that the guests knew the location, where to park and gave them an arrival time and a dress code (internal and external resources). She checked that Joy's health was up to such a night (ecology). Linda created an image in her mind of the guests leaving the restaurant smiling and laughing, and Joy sitting happily at the table having had a wonderful evening (sensory-based evidence). The schedule of things to do before the event helped it run smoothly and allowed Linda to enjoy the evening as much as Joy (timing). A hostess with real purpose and drive! Consider the consequences of not having well-formed outcomes to achieve her goal. She might have left preparations to the last minute; found Joy's favourite restaurant to be fully booked; spent the hours before the event taking phone calls from guests needing directions; feeling bad and apologizing to Joy for not having booked her favourite restaurant; and arrived in a flustered state unable to give Joy and her guests attention.

Everyday experiences like this make a big difference to your energy and results. Taking the PRIEST approach opens up future possibilities. Linda's reputation for organizing events calmly and effectively is a skill that she applies to other areas of her life, including her work and family. When you work with outcomes in this way you will generate positive energy that will attract positive people to you.

Despite an underprivileged upbringing, Tom has an unstoppable sense of purpose. Combining his skills as an expressive dancer with his ability to teach dance as a way of helping youngsters to be confident and to believe in themselves, he embarked on a mission. When we met Tom he had a very clear out-come. He wanted to establish a dancing competition which enabled teams from schools around London to design and perform their own dance creations. They would then enter a series of qualifying events and the teams chosen for the final would have the opportunity to dance on stage at Olympia. His out-come was clear. He took on the role of organizer and his values around young people and creative expression held him in good stead. He worked on his self-belief and quickly acquired internal resources of confidence and determination to turn the idea into a series of actions. From there on he knew where to find the external resources he needed and took control of the entire project. Tom knew exactly what he would hear, see and feel when the event was success-ful. Six months later hundreds of highly expressive youngsters took to the stage at the first Olympiada ever in the UK. It was a great success.

Putting everything together to create a brilliant future

If you have followed all the exercises in this book you now have every-thing you need to create a brilliant future for yourself. The next exercise gives you a structure for choosing whatever techniques are appropriate to make desired changes. It can be used in conjunction with the PRIEST exercise, or on its own as a way of becoming aligned with a personal change you want to make. It is used here along with the PRIEST exercise. As you proceed there are suggested techniques you may wish to use, some of which you have covered in previous sections of the book, others are in the compendium section at the end.

Creating a brilliant future

1. Prepare a set of cards or sheets of paper marked as follows.

Identity

Values & beliefs

Capability

Behaviour

Environment

2. Sit in a quiet place, relax and look up. Create an image of what life will be like at some point in the future. Choose a period when you have achieved one or more outcomes that are important to you now.

3. Mark two spots on the floor – one to represent today and one for a time in the future when you will have achieved a specific outcome. The distance (time) between the two spots is what feels right. Stand on the future spot and imagine what it is like. Imagine you have a remote control like the one you use on your television set. Use it to intensify the qualities of your internal imagery and sound. Turn up

▶

the brightness, increase the colour, improve the contrast, make it bigger and bring it closer. Turn up the volume and listen to the sounds. Have the sound well tuned so there is no interference. Step into the picture and notice the feelings of satisfaction and achievement. Enjoy the moment and anchor this state.

Techniques used

- Anchoring

4. Put your cards at equal intervals, in the order shown above, between where you are standing now ('future') and the spot representing 'today'.

5. Stand at a point just beyond the future spot and look back to 'today'. Fire the anchor you set earlier. How does it feel having achieved your outcome(s)? From this position, what have you got to say to the you of 'today'? Have you any tips or advice?

6. Move to the 'identity' card. Ask yourself how you have changed now that you have achieved your outcome(s). What is different about you? What role are you now playing that you were not playing before?

7. Move to the 'Values & beliefs' card. What values have you changed, if any, and how have your beliefs changed in order to achieve this success?

Techniques used

- Values elicitation
- Belief change
- Reframing
- *This* not *that*
- Metamodel.

8. Move to the 'Capability' spot. How have your capabilities changed? What did you learn along the way?

Techniques used

■ Artfully vague language.

9. Move to the 'Behaviour' card. What did you do along the way? What are you doing differently now?

Techniques used

■ New behaviour generator (in compendium section)

■ Collapsing anchors

■ Anchoring

■ PRIEST

■ Strategies.

10. Move on to the 'Environment' card. What impact has achieving your outcome(s) had on those around you? Is your environment still the same or has it changed in any way? If so how?

Technique used

■ Perceptual positions (in compendium section)

11. Revisit the cards in any order you wish if you feel that there is still work to do. You will know when you have true alignment – when all the tugs have disappeared and you have a burning desire to make your first move.

Spacing the exercise out on the floor helps you to 'programme in' the changes you want to make and gives you a better concept of space and time than if you were to do the exercise mentally. If you have completed the exercise correctly there is no need to write anything down – you should have integrated it firmly and clearly.

9 Adopting the beliefs on which NLP is based

Now that you have some experience of NLP, adopting the beliefs on which it is founded will expedite your journey to success. NLP was originally used to model excellence. The following beliefs were modelled from people who excelled in their field. They are referred to as the 'presuppositions' of NLP.

The map is not the territory

You have your own unique understanding of the world around you. However, how you perceive it isn't how it actually is! You can never have ALL the information ALL the time. Just as a map doesn't show every house, shop, tree or bump in the road, your map is merely your representation of the world, rather than reality.

You create your map by filtering information through your senses, the language you use, your beliefs and values, and your experience.

Respect others' maps of the world

Developing a state of curiosity is one of the most useful states you can achieve if you are going to communicate successfully. If everyone's map is different who is to say who has the right one or the best one? An effective state of curiosity will allow you to gain information about the other person's map, which will help you to build rapport, communicate and influence. An effective state of curiosity includes a healthy respect for other people's maps. It does not mean you have to agree, but it is useful to understand.

The meaning of your communication is the response you get

Taking responsibility for your communication will give you control over the process and the results. It is common for people to give their view of something and then blame others or circumstances when they are not understood. If you want control over your success then take responsibility for your communication – if you don't get the response you expected first time then try explaining differently.

If it's possible for one person, it's possible for others

You have all the resources you need to make changes in your life. In situations where you find yourself struggling to achieve, it's not that you don't have the internal resources, it's just that you are in an unresourceful state. Developing resourceful states is crucial to the pursuit of success. You can achieve anything you decide – but some things will take longer than others. Be sure to check the consequences of dedicating your life to achieving your aspirations.

There is no failure, only feedback

If what you do isn't creating the desired result, you have still created *a* result. Use the feedback you get to explore what you can do differently to get the outcome you want. Ask yourself 'What can I learn from this?' and 'What can I do differently?' Focus on solutions and what else is possible, rather than on problems. Failure exists only as a state of mind – a perception.

Mind and body are part of the same system

The way you think has a direct impact on your physiology. If your thoughts are making you feel sad then your body will reflect this. If your thoughts are making you feel happy then your body will reflect this. Negative thinking has a tendency to cause stress and tension, blocking energy flow – it is increasingly recognized that serious illnesses can be caused by the build-up of stress. It makes sense to keep energy flowing by thinking positively.

Every behaviour has a positive intention

You make the best choices you can with the resources available at the time. The intention in your choice is a positive one for you, even though others may not see it that way.

> Ben chose not to telephone a girl he met at a party the previous evening, even though they had got on really well and that she had been delighted when he asked for her telephone number. Past experience of relationships with girls told Ben he would get hurt. His behaviour had a positive intention to protect him from perceived hurt. The girl was disappointed.

The person with the most flexibility will control the system

In systems thinking this is known as 'the law of requisite variety'. Flexibility of thinking and behaviour will give you the advantage in understanding other people's maps of reality, build rapport and achieve outcomes. Being too fixed and rigid can create a stalemate situation where no desired outcomes are achieved and can also restrict the number of people you can build rapport with. Flexibility does not mean giving way to every idea but being able to adapt and pace and lead with your thinking and behaviour. Inflexibility is narrow-mindedness, having fixed ideas and 'one way of doing things'.

If you always do what you've always done, you'll always get what you've always had

Unconscious programming causes you to repeat patterns, even though you are aware they are not working. Until you learn to reprogramme your thinking your results are unlikely to change change.

Your behaviour is not who you are

A behaviour is something you do which is given meaning by other people. In other words, people make their own interpretations of your behaviour by using their own map as a measure. Chances are that their interpretation is inaccurate. Successful people remember to look beyond behaviour in their interactions with people.

Your perception is your reality

Your map of reality is created by the way you perceive things. Your perception of a situation will be different from that of, say, your next-door neighbour or your partner, offspring, manager or colleague. On the basis that no two people can possibly have exactly the same experience, there are very few universal truths.

You are in charge of your mind, and therefore your results

Everything starts with one thought. If you are in control of your thoughts you are in control of your behaviour, and therefore your results.

Resistance is a sign of a lack of rapport

After you have taken the trouble to build rapport with someone you can lead and pace them to a win–win outcome. When rapport is absent there will be signs of resistance – for example, the person will carry on with what they were doing while you are talking, or there will be mismatches in your body posture. Without rapport win–win outcomes are unlikely to be achieved.

You cannot not communicate

In the 1960s Professor Albert Mehrabian conducted some research into the effectiveness of spoken communication. It resulted in the following statistics:

- 7% of meaning is in the words that are spoken
- 38% of meaning is in the way the words are said
- 55% of meaning is in body language and facial expression.

Although these statistics are approximate – and are distorted when the telephone is being used – they highlight the importance of facial expression, body language and tone of voice in the communication process. Whatever you do, even if you think you are sitting quietly minding your own business, someone will be attaching meaning to your behaviour.

You have all the resources you need to change

Believing this will help you to help yourself and others to find the resources you need to make changes that will serve you well.

10 A compendium of additional NLP techniques

Perceptual positions

Use this technique to understand other people's maps of reality and reach mutually beneficial agreements. For example, when preparing for meetings, dealing with family members including children, in customer care, selling, negotiating, coaching and giving presentations.

When rapport is low and you are not getting along with someone you want to influence, it helps if you can see the relationship from their point of view. The ability to look at an issue from a number of different perspectives can greatly add to the amount of information you have, and help you to make better decisions and choices.

As well as seeing things from others' perspectives it is even more useful to hear and feel things too. By acting as if you are someone else you can begin to understand some of their beliefs, values and representations, and gain a more complete understanding of how they might behave and react to the things you say and do. It enables you to understand others more and to expand your own level of awareness. The following exercise is designed to help you to gain a perspective on any given situation from three angles.

1. Think of a situation you are going to face in the near future, that causes you some anxiety or apprehension.

2. You are going to view the situation from three different angles. Set a scene as though you are getting ready for a play using props such as chairs and tables.

3. *First position (You)* – in this position consider things only from your own point of view. You want to know how things affect you and how you feel. This first position is really useful when you want to assert yourself, check out how you feel about a situation or outcome, and ensure that your needs are met.

   Staying here all the time, however, is unhelpful since you will have little, or no, awareness of your impact on others, or of their needs and preferences, and you may jump to conclusions without fully checking them out.

4. *Second position (the other person's shoes)* – physically put yourself in the position of the other person in your scene. From here you can look back at yourself in the first position, step in to the other person's shoes and experience things the way they do. This is more than thinking 'what you would do if you were them'. It is about projecting 'you' into 'him or her' and really understanding their perspective to gain more accurate information. What is their role? What are their priorities? What pressure are they under? What values and beliefs are driving their behaviour?

   Adopting this position gives you a better understanding of the other person's behaviour and map of reality and, how they perceive you.

5. *Third position (fly on the wall)* – now stand away from the scene so that you can see yourself in the first position and the other person in the second. From here you take the role of an independent observer,

detached and dissociated from the other two positions. Imagine you are a film director or a fly-on-the-wall documentary producer. You are observing from a logical, rational and objective perspective. In this position you may notice what both parties can do differently to improve the relationship and achieve a win–win outcome.

6. Revisit any of the positions to gain further understanding.

All three positions are equally valuable. By carrying out this exercise in real space and time you can increase your understanding, increase your chances of building better rapport, create new ideas and solutions and open up new ways of thinking.

The swish technique

Use this technique to change a habit – for example nail biting, skin picking, clock watching, poor performance in sport, road rage, eating habits (identify specific triggers such as comfort eating or excitement). You can also use it to change your response to something – for example from 'immediate' to 'considered', from 'aggressive' to 'assertive'.

1. Choose a past negative situation where you demonstrated the behaviour you want to change. Create a fully associated image in your mind. Focus on what happened. Put a frame around the image. Identify one or two qualities of your internal image that, when intensified, change your internal response – you will probably notice this change as a feeling. Usually the brightness and size work best, but colour, contrast, location or depth may work also. Play around with this until you are happy with the chosen qualities.

2. Change your state by taking some deep breaths and stretching.

3. Create an unframed image in your mind of the behaviour you would like to have instead. Really see yourself doing it. Make your picture dissociated – you are looking at yourself in the picture. Dissociated pictures create the motivation for moving towards something you want. Include all the resources you will need – strength, confidence, clarity of thought, listening ability, creativity, focus, relaxation, humour. Make your image compelling and realistic, and check it out with respect to other areas of your life. Try it out for different contexts – is this 'new you' ecological with other relationships? If you were to respond in this way in different contexts would the outcome be favourable to you and those you interact with? You may want to alter the image so that you are completely happy with it. When you are happy with it intensify it and make it really compelling.

4. Shrink this image down to the size of a postage stamp, allowing the colour to drain out of it, and all the sounds to become dull and muted.

5. Change your state.

6. Take your first image and increase the two strongest qualities you chose in step 1. Now take your new self-image that you have shrunk, and put it in the bottom corner of your first image. The next step

should be done quickly –as you say to yourself 'swish', instantaneously make the large picture small and dark, while making the new self-image large and bright. They swap places instantly and the negative image disappears completely.

Swish Technique

7. Repeat step 6 about five times, making sure that you change your state by taking some deep breaths and stretching between each one. Speed and repetition are essential.

8. Test your new response by imagining a time in the future when you will want this different response. This is called 'future pacing'. If you still get the original response, go back to step 1 and repeat the exercise. You will know when you have been successful because you will no longer be able to bring back the negative image.

New behaviour generator

Use this technique to create an entirely new behaviour.

1. With your eyes down to the left, ask yourself 'If I were able to . . . (state your goal) . . . what would I look like?'

2. With eyes up to the right, construct a visual image of what you would look like if you were in the act of achieving your goal. Construct the image from a dissociated point of view.

3. Mentally step inside the image so that you now feel yourself doing what you just saw yourself doing in the image. What do you see, hear and feel?

4. Compare the feelings you have with the feelings from a similar experience in which you were successful.

5. If the two feelings match then you have finished.

6. If the two feelings don't match then name what is missing – creativity, more confidence, be more relaxed etc.

7. Refine your goal statement by adding 'and . . . (the additional resource(s) you have chosen).'

8. Go back to step 1 and repeat the exercise.

Visual squash

Use this technique to resolve conflicting beliefs or values in yourself. The trigger here is generally when you hear yourself saying 'Part of me wants to do/believes X and part of me wants to do/believes Y.

1. Identify conflicting beliefs or wants.

2. Create a visual representation of each part, one in each hand, and hold them out in front of you.

3. Identify an outcome and ask for agreement from both parts.

4. Ask each part for its positive intention and continue chunking up to high-level values until you reach an agreement.

5. Have each part look at the other and say what it sees and thinks. Include resources, strengths, beliefs and expectations.

6. Ask both parts to state their readiness to give and receive resources, or to negotiate if necessary.

7. Bring both hands together and pull both parts inside you to integrate them within you. They should do so willingly.

8. Check for objections from any other parts. If there are any objections then do the exercise again with the objecting part present. Put this new part on a chair where you can relate to it from a distance.

Conclusion

NLP is a skill that requires practice and your journey through this book is the first step towards a better life. We trust you have enjoyed it and encourage you to continue practising the techniques you found most useful on a daily basis. Through practice you develop confidence, and over time new ways of thinking and behaving will come to you naturally.

Remember – being stuck with programmes that are limiting you is a choice. NLP gives you tools that make it easy for you to exercise more choice about the way you experience life. Choose well.

How to contact the authors

David Molden – david@quadrant1.com
Pat Hutchinson – pat@quadrant1.com
Website – www.quadrant1.com